Ada

An Account of the Ada LeBoeuf - Thomas Dreher Murder Case

by
Charles M. Hargroder

Published by
The Center for Louisiana Studies
University of Louisiana at Lafayette
Lafayette, Louisiana

Cover Photo
St. Mary Parish Courthouse and jail at the time of the
LeBoeuf - Dreher Trial

Library of Congress Catalog Number: 99-76957
ISBN Number: 1-887366-35-0

Published by The Center for Louisiana Studies
P.O. Box 40831
University of Louisiana at Lafayette
Lafayette, LA 70504-0831

Contents

For

Rivers E. Hargroder

Foreword

It was a brutal murder, but where was the evidence other than conflicting confessions and testimony by Ada LeBoeuf, Dr. Thomas Dreher, and the trapper, James Beadle, who later recanted? Then, there was the post-sentence petition by eleven of the twelve convicting jurors asking clemency to replace the death sentence with life imprisonment.

Ada and Dr. Dreher were identified in newspapers as lovers, a point never explored as a motive by the prosecution and raised only by attorneys (without proof) for Beadle, a codefendant.

Yet, Mrs. LeBoeuf and Dr. Dreher were found guilty and sentenced to hang, touching off an almost hysterical public appeal for clemency. Nevertheless, the pair were executed, the first time in 116 years of statehood that Louisiana had sent a woman to the gallows. The LeBoeuf-Dreher murder case thus became a part of Louisiana's rich and colorful past.

The author was born one block from the courthouse square the year before the trial which attracted international attention, and he grew up hearing fragments of the case. His interest was piqued by the fact that the physician at his birth also had been the coroner in the case and that the presiding judge was a friend of his mother's family.

A frequent visitor to family in the Teche country, the writer was and is familiar with the area described herein—Morgan City, the ferry, the route from there to Franklin and points between, the graveled road bordering the bayou, Dr. Aycock's Patterson hospital, the Williams lodge and airport (from which he witnessed flight of an early version of the autogiro), the magnificent old St. Mary Parish Courthouse, damaged by a hurricane and now replaced by a modern structure with none of the grace of the old one, and Franklin, in particular. Those scenes recounted in this book are drawn from personal memory.

Descriptions of Mrs. LeBoeuf, Dr. Dreher, and James Beadle were obtained from news stories of the time. Those stories also were the basis for description of the crime scene, and the discovery of the body and the subsequent autopsy report.

James LeBoeuf's maltreatment of his wife is recorded in Milton Mackaye's account of the murder, published in *Dramatic Crimes of 1927: A*

Study in Mystery and Detection. They are attributed to comments to reporters by Mrs. Noah (Rosalie) Hebert, a confidant of Mrs. LeBoeuf, and to Mrs. LeBoeuf's brother-in-law, Morgan City Police Chief Louis Blakeman.

Accounts of the arrest and initial questioning of both Mrs. LeBoeuf and Dr. Dreher are taken from the trial transcript, as well as news stories, and comments from the district attorney to newsmen. Other quotations throughout the book are taken from trial transcript or from news stories.

The writer is indebted to Mr. Ashton Phelps, Jr., publisher of the *New Orleans Times-Picayune,* for permission to use extensive quotes from reporters covering the case; to the staff of the Louisiana Collection, Louisiana State Library, for their assistance; to the St. Mary Parish clerk of court's office for access to the transcript of the trial; to the staff of the Morgan City Archives for certain materials and information; to Herb R. Graf, Ph D., for helpful suggestions as to sources, and to Damon Veach for initial reading of the manuscript and genealogical help.

1

There it was again, "clickity, clickity, clickity," like the sound of a score of knitting needles, but without rhythm. It came feverishly in the tar black, moonless night, the ebony darkness enveloping all .in an almost suffocating embrace. In the tropic heat, the air was more moisture than ether. Breathing came almost in gulps.

A small gasoline engine powered skiff bobbed in the shallow water lapping against the nearby mud bank, a remnant of the slowly receding spring flood which had swept down the Mississippi and Atchafalaya rivers. Though it was midsummer, the water still drained through the swamp to Lake Palourde and channeled to the Gulf of Mexico.

Palourde was a tidewater lake, its currents ebbing and flowing with tides in the gulf. The brackish water sustaining crabs, shrimp, and oysters as well as reptilian life such as alligators. Now the water licked the edges of the mud bank, a gentle slosh muffled against the sides of the boat, masking the sound of oars as three men maneuvered their skiff closer toward the bank.

One man wielded a flashlight, sweeping a yellow beam seeking out frogs that croaked ceaselessly. One of his companions was half crouched near the prow of the boat, his arm holding a gig ready to spear them. The clicking stopped as the boat scraped its shallow draft bottom against the mud flat. This craft required more water than the swamp pirogue which natives said could navigate even a heavy dew. With a thud, the boat jolted into something more solid than mud.

John Beadle was in the prow. His cousin, Cleveland Beadle, was amidships, and in the stern sat Alcide Mayon, their friend. All three were trappers by vocation, but in this off-season, they were hunting frogs which brought a good price in New Orleans restaurants. John steadied himself as his flashlight illuminated the obstacle, apparently snagged by a submerged tree branch, three, perhaps four feet beneath the lake's surface. The beam revealed a mass of what he first took to be the water-whitened carcass of an animal.

When the light caught it, crabs scurried in every direction for shelter, disturbed in their feeding. It was their claws tearing at flesh as they feasted on morsels they brought to the surface that was the clicking the trappers had heard. It was not unusual to come across decaying animal and vegetable matter in this torrid July heat. It was more the norm in the weeks of early summer in 1927 as continuing drainoff from the great flood earlier in the year revealed new silt deposits. But this stench was abnormally malodorous. With his gig, Cleveland poked at the dead creature while John concentrated a beam of light on it.

It was the body of a man, and he had been severely mutilated, as the natives would say, "carved like a pig." Cleveland moved in closer, and Alcide stood up to get a better look. There in the water was what was left of a human body, only the back and hips exposed, clad in a long-sleeved white shirt, an undershirt, and light blue pants drawn down over the knees. His face had been badly disfigured by the crabs and fish.

None of the three men could identify the corpse, but from the severe and extensive cuts on the body, they knew he had been murdered—those injuries were no accident. Further examination showed railroad angle irons had been suspended around his neck by a half-inch rope, tied with a double hitch, his feet similarly tied and weighted by the same materials.

Someone had not wanted the body found. That was especially evident by the way the body had been disemboweled in what looked like an attempt to prevent a buildup of bodily gasses which would have caused the corpse normally to surface within days. That someone had not counted on the current of the lake as waters dropped, snagging the body in shallow water rather than nudging it into the deeper channel leading to the gulf. Had the body been dumped 50 feet further out, it probably would have been submerged 100 feet beneath the surface of the muddy water rather than the three to four feet just off the mud bank. This was clearly a matter for law enforcement officials.

Louis B. Blakeman was chief of the small Morgan City police force. While he had no jurisdiction over the murder scene, he was the only "law" the men knew to be close by. When the trapper trio reached town, they went to Blakeman's home, banged at the door, and roused the lawman from his sleep. Blakeman, once fully awake, phoned Dr. C. C. DeGravelles, the assistant parish coroner. This was more his domain. Within half an hour, a small armada arrived at the spot where the trappers had found the body. Although it was barely dawn, the men DeGravelles had recruited to help in recovering the body were sweating and straining as they lifted it into a boat. Only as they raised the cadaver to the boat's rim did they realize that the weight came from angle irons, estimated later to weigh about 150 pounds.

DeGravelles decided to move the investigation to a local mortuary and the flotilla returned to Morgan City, about one mile distant. From there, he called the parish coroner, Dr. C. M. Horton, his boss, at Franklin, the parish seat some 25 miles away. He reported to Horton what appeared to be a criminal matter. After brief conversation in which Horton said he would be on the scene as soon as possible, it was agreed that DeGravelles would attempt to identify the victim in the meantime. It didn't take long. Charlie Garber, who lived down the street from the dead man, identified the body as that of James LeBoeuf, superintendent of the Morgan City Power and Light, missing for six days.

Charles Burgers said he recognized the corpse as LeBoeuf by the shoes he still wore—water soaked tan oxfords with new heels. The reason he said he knew those shoes was that LeBoeuf had showed them to him several days before he disappeared. He had just had new heels put on.

Police Chief Blakeman was also able to identify the dead man. He said he had known LeBoeuf for 23 years. After all, the man was his brother-in-law for 20 years. He should know him. Strange that Jim's wife, Ada, had not reported him missing, She had passed off his absence as probably an out-of-town trip to the Lafayette or Texas headquarters of Louisiana Power & Light, parent company of the Morgan City utility company. He frequently did that. Blakeman had checked out that possibility, but no one at the Lafayette office had seen LeBoeuf. There the matter stood until now.

2

Sleepily the little town was awakening. Some of the inhabitants were already headed to the wharf to select fish for the table. In the more prosperous part of town, heavily perspiring maids attacked the family laundry, generously applying hard, yellow lye soap as they rubbed the clothes across heavy scrubboards. Steam rose from water in large black iron sugar kettles, several feet in diameter, long unused for their original purpose, now utilized as laundry tubs, the water heated from beneath by wood fires.

Many of the women had brought along their children who helped by swirling the clothing in the kettles with long wooden poles, lifting items at intervals with the pole into smaller galvanized tubs for scrubbing. Those who rose earlier had a head start against the day's heat, already rinsing heavier bed linens and hanging them on clotheslines to dry and bleach in the scorching sun.

Vegetable and fruit wagons eased down the few passable inundated residential streets. "I got fresh bananas 10 cents a dozen," called one vendor. "Nice fresh shelled cow peas, creole tomatoes just picked this morning." Others hawked shallots, okra, corn, and cucumbers. Most of the vendors carried containers by which to measure peas and beans, already shelled for customer convenience, which they sold by the cup.

In their wake came a small open-backed truck, its canvas top and side insulating burlap-wrapped bulk ice, some pre-cut in small blocks easily handled by brawny men swinging scissor-like ice tongs. A deft throw and the sharp pincers gripped the amount ordered by the householder. Ten cents for the smaller block, 25 cents for a larger piece hopefully lasting in insulated iceboxes until the ice man came again the next day.

Morgan City was a relatively treeless little town, although spaced around the homes were some live oaks, catalpa trees, with their large leaves and white clusters of trumpet-shaped flowers, and spreading chinaberry trees scattering their yellow, pulpy, bead-like fruit over lawns.

Barefoot boys climbed the chinaberry trees to select the green balls before they ripened into mushy yellow. They used them as ammunition for their slingshots. Meanwhile, little girls skipped perilously close to the light pink "snake flowers" edging open roadside drainage ditches. It was not that snakes were attracted to the flowers, but the flowers grew in areas where snakes were found.

Front yards were filled with rose of Sharon and frothy crape myrtles in shades of watermelon red, pink, lavender, and white clusters of tiny crinkled blossoms. An afternoon rain with even a slight breeze would coat the ground beneath with fallen delicate petals.

Backyard fig trees bore an abundant crop in the rainy season which was harvested early in morning before blue jays ate their fill, pecking away at only enough of the fruit as to spoil it for human consumption. If left unharvested, the remnants soured, leaving a sickly sweet stench.

Rear yards were demarcated by gray, weathered wooden fences in poorer sections of town, white-washed paling in the more prosperous neighborhoods, constructed low enough that womenfolk could exchange local gossip across them, a common form of recreation, whether it was benign or malicious.

Near the center of town was a park roughly two blocks long. At one end was a large gazebo which sometimes served as a bandstand, and live oaks spread to cover a nearby slide, swings, seesaw, a small carousel, and a sandbox. A large treeless open area bordered by tall palms mostly was used by young adults for softball.

The town already had begun to bake under a tireless sun, endlessly reflecting its heat off those clam shell-paved streets beginning to protrude above receding floodwater, producing a white glare that made it seem that much hotter. From mid-morning until late afternoon adults took refuge behind dark green shuttered windows, keeping high-ceilinged interiors in near darkness throughout the day. Those who moved around in the searing heat did so under cover of black parasols moving like a stream of spoiled mushrooms along blanched white pathways emerging from the water.

Morgan City, located on Berwick Bay near the confluence of Bayou Teche and the Atchafalaya River, had a population of roughly 5,500 with another 1,500 on the Berwick side of the bay. This population was made up primarily of migrant hunters, fishermen, and trappers. A majority of these were French-speaking descendants of Acadian exiles, immortalized in Longfellow's *Evangeline,* and now called Cajuns. Their language was not pure French, but a patois, derived of the language of Paris when their ancestors fled Europe to avoid religious persecution, punctuated by English for words for which they knew no equivalent in French. They lived largely on the bounty of muskrat, alligator, and other animal furs and hides taken from the huge primeval Atchafalaya swamp, waterlogged home of several Indian tribes which first inhabited it and which extended almost fifty miles north and west of the town. Intermixed and inter-married among the Cajuns were people of German, English, and Italian ancestry.

Directly across the bay was Berwick, which, like Patterson further up the Teche, was home port to a fleet of individually owned small trawlers, regularly venturing into the gulf in pursuit of shrimp, crab, and other seafood.

On high land of rich black loam bordering the Teche for miles to the west, sugarcane planters reaped rich harvest. Morgan City itself was once part of a large sugarcane plantation. Now it was the hub of water-borne commerce as barges pushed by motor-driven tugs plied the Atchafalaya River and bayou country, vying with the railroad for small freight service west to St. Martinville and on to Lafayette.

The backyard grapevine quickly disseminated news of the grisly lake find through the community and, like in any retelling of events, scraps of gossip were repeated as gospel. The gossip mill inevitably churned out stories of the marital relations of the deceased and his widow.

The LeBoeufs were respectable members of the community, of modest station. They had three sons and a daughter who was the youngest, patriotically named Liberty, born in the aftermath of the Great War. The eldest son, Joseph, was already earning a livelihood, though still residing with his parents. His younger brother, Ernest, the most handsome of the boys, was captain of the football team at Morgan City High School where he would be a senior in the fall. Herman, the youngest son, was an average 12-year-old boy.

LeBoeuf, lacking a formal education, was self-made and industrious. He had been a farmer, a teamster, an engineer in the local ice factory, and finally manager of the Morgan City utility company before it was acquired by Louisiana Power & Light, which made him their superintendent. The LeBoeufs lived in an unpretentious part of town in a two-story clapboard house, its long-weathered paint giving a shabby appearance, but it was still better than many of their neighbors' homes.

Like the lazy surface of a bayou, Ada and Jim appeared to be comfortably wed. Like the bayou, though, beneath the surface all was not tranquil. Jim LeBoeuf was a jealous man of quick temper. He often beat Ada during a jealous rage, and as a result, Ada would not appear in public to engage in any activity which could spark another of his outbursts. As evidence of Jim's violence, Ada frequently had purple bruises peeping from under short-sleeved dresses.

LeBoeuf's neighbors knew him to be a jealous man, his vigilance to be that of a sick man, even distrustful of Ada's few women friends who trod lightly under his dark scrutiny whenever they visited. Despite this, LeBoeuf was considered to be a pillar of the community, active in civic affairs, and a social associate of men like Dr. Thomas E. Dreher, who had moved to Morgan City shortly after the turn of the century from the Baton Rouge area and established a thriving medical practice, augmented by a prosperous drug company.

LeBoeuf and Dreher were frequent hunting companions, and in time they became close friends. On the other hand, Dr. Dreher's wife, a well-educated woman of refinement and culture, had differing interests than Jim's wife, Ada, so that the two women moved in different social circles. The Drehers had a grown son, called Ted (a derivative of his initials—Thomas E. Dreher, Jr.), a student at Tulane University, his father's alma mater, and two daughters, Dorothy, 19, and Polly, 15.

Over time, Dreher and LeBoeuf included a third party in their hunting and fishing expeditions, a trapper, James Beadle, who referred to himself as a guide. A swarthy Cajun, Beadle was the best shot of the three. He had the reputation of having a short fuse and an explosive temper.

Eventually the convivial relationship between LeBoeuf and Beadle soured. They never revealed the cause of the rift, but locals said that LeBoeuf once borrowed a skiff from Beadle without first asking permission. Beadle had planned to use the boat the same day. Finding it gone, he discovered it had been taken by LeBoeuf. His Cajun temper flaring, Beadle vowed he would kill LeBoeuf on his return. Unaware of the turmoil he had caused, LeBoeuf fortunately left the boat further down the bayou, thus unwittingly avoiding a confrontation. That gossip may or may not have been the cause of the rift, but the pair never shared hunting and fishing trips again.

Dreher and Beadle retained their relationship. Beadle considered himself an employee, loyal to the doctor who often was the economic backbone of the trapper, his wife, and seven children. Some said that Beadle would do anything Dreher wanted—say hop and he would jump.

The town did not immediately recognize things for what they later assumed them to be. The doctor was physician to the LeBoeuf family and came and went to the LeBoeuf home during LeBoeuf's out-of-town business trips. All seemed well and proper. Still, every small town has its meddlers, one of whom wrote an anonymous letter to Mrs. Dreher containing an accusation of illicit relations between Dr. Dreher and Ada LeBoeuf. Not knowing what to do or believe, Mrs. Dreher took the letter to LeBoeuf at his office. Without this flash point igniting an already suspicious LeBoeuf, perhaps the conflagration that followed never would have been.

Jim LeBoeuf's nature confirmed the story as far as he was concerned. First he accosted Ada and accused her of infidelity. It was a frightful scene, with Jim finally beating his wife, causing blood to flow from a severe blow to the nose. Standing over her as she lay on the floor, he swore "If ever I can prove what I suspect about you and Dr. Dreher, I'll kill you."

The gossips gloried in every morsel that circulated. Some said that a pillowcase seen airing over the window ledge of Ada's bedroom was a signal to Dr. Dreher that her husband was at home.

LeBoeuf, they said, was so beside himself with distrust that one evening he donned some of his wife's clothes, and drove around town in the hope that Dreher would, from a distance, mistake him for his wife, and approach and perhaps give him reason to blast him with the shotgun he carried by his side.

His mistrust soared to such levels that he went to his brother-in-law, Police Chief Blakeman, demanding that Dreher be prevented from driving past his home.

"I can't keep a man off a public street!" Blakeman told the fuming LeBoeuf. Then, Blakeman subsequently told others, LeBoeuf threatened to kill his wife. As Blakeman later said, LeBoeuf told him that if Dreher ever attempted to contact or see his wife again, he would kill him, too.

The morning Jim LeBoeuf's body was found, as townsfolk "happened by" the corner at Shannon's Hardware on Railroad Avenue and Front Street and others "just found themselves" at the ferry landing at the foot of Frerett Street, speculation based on all this hearsay was runaway.

3

The two middle-aged men sat at the table overlooking the bay, slowly sipping their coffee, with nowhere to go until the ferry came. Overhead fans made the wait more bearable, as had the late breakfast. Foote's Restaurant was famous for its good food and this morning was no exception. When they had arrived at the restaurant, Sheriff Charles Pecot had suspected it was purposeful that they just missed a departure of the ferry so that his companion could have breakfast.

Both Pecot and the coroner, Dr. Charles M. Horton, wore lightweight suits, although the sheriff had left his coat in the car. He wore navy blue suspenders, but really didn't need them to hold up his trousers. Both men were showing early signs of rumpling under the onslaught of heat and moisture. But that was the beauty of Palm Beach suits, their ability to withstand Louisiana summers and still maintain an acceptable appearance. In the restaurant's informal atmosphere they did not remove their hats.

Pecot wore his stiff straw boater slightly cocked off his forehead, his tie loosened at the neck. He was big and broad, a man accustomed to being obeyed, a man direct and straightforward but with a courtly manner not uncommon in this French-speaking part of the country.

The sheriff had held his office for about eleven years. Before that he had been chief of police at Franklin, then was a deputy to two prior sheriffs. He suspected the case he was about to investigate would be the messiest in his experience as a lawman, but as a lawman he felt he should look forward to it. He didn't because he knew intuitively that it would involve local people, people he had known since childhood, or with whom he had socialized, and who perhaps were political supporters. Moreover, no matter what he knew was his obligation to uphold the law, there were times that his personal inclination was to take sides in a situation.

Sitting with him was his chief deputy, W. J. Blunt, and the parish coroner, also a man of many years service in the Teche area. They had been associated in criminal investigations before, but knew each other more intimately as neighbors in Franklin and as members of the Knights of Columbus.

Horton had delivered more babies in the Teche country than anyone, physician or midwife. Because of the area's predominant Acadian heritage, probably most children were born with his help, although they later came under his care when medical help was required. He sat savoring an unlighted cigar clutched between his teeth. Doc Horton seldom smoked, but he appreciated the aroma of a good cigar. Perspiration, despite the fans, trickled down his forehead undeflected by the sweatband in his Panama straw. He had an almost cherubic countenance, made more so by plump cheeks and a pleasant expression, and an ever-present twinkle in his blue eyes.

Blunt, an undistinguished man in his late twenties, seemed uncomfortable in a shirt and tie. He had hung his coat over the back of his chair, and his shirt hung a little snug and damp across his broad shoulders, and a stiff straw hat slouched back on his head like the sheriff's.

From where the trio sat, they could see the ferry churning across red-brown Berwick Bay. The waters were slightly choppy, and glistened under a cloudless sky. Toward their right they could see the Southern Pacific railway bridge.

Foote's, although located at the foot of where U. S. Highway 90 was interrupted by the bay, was not named for its location, but for A. N. Foote, the owner. The restaurant was noted for its Cajun cuisine and drew its clientele from miles around. Already the staff was preparing for the lunch crowd, and the steamy kitchen was emitting a spicy aroma.

Miss Jenny (some called her Big Mama because of her girth) busied herself and the staff that waited tables to assure the settings were ready for a rapid turnover. She had their tab ready for the trio as they lumbered up from their table and prepared to go get in their car while the westbound traffic cleared the ferry landing. A gentle breeze swept over the bay offsetting the heat as the three men sat in the open touring car, thankful they had ridden over in it rather than a closed vehicle. Once in Morgan City, Horton went to the funeral home where LeBoeuf's body had been taken. Sheriff Pecot went to the office of Chief of Police Blakeman.

There was a knot of the curious outside the white clapboard pier and beam structure, a former store, the undertaker's name inscribed in black on wide glass windows. The exterior was stained by the recent flood. Open weave lace curtains shielded the interior, framed by dusty velvet drapes which had once been a richer hue of purple. Whirring standing pedestal fans stirred the air in the outer reception room, whipping around the omnipresent smell of embalming fluid and recent floral offerings. The lighting was dim and directed upward at the ceiling. To the rear, through an archway was the "waking room" in which about a dozen men were milling in clusters. Horton assumed these included the coroner's jury and witnesses. Farther back was the embalming room where Horton was told the remains lay. He quickly made his way there and closed the door.

The body before him was apparently that of a middle-aged white man, coatless, in a once-white shirt made dingy by days in muddy water. The shirt had powder-burns where two loads of buckshot had entered the side. He also wore light blue pants with a small darker blue stripe and still wore a pair of tan shoes.

The victim had a peculiarly shaped thumb (one was missing) and his upper and lower dentures were intact. The body had a long abdominal incision, one which would appear to have been the handiwork of a trained surgeon, but equally could have been made by a hunter seasoned in field dressing his kill. The feet and neck had been relieved of the railroad angle irons which had weighted the corpse.

After a brief examination, the corner presented his findings to the jury. He explained that the victim was about 145 pounds, and provided additional observations. Details of where and how the body had been found were offered by Mayon and the two Beadle cousins.

"When we found him," Cleveland Beadle testified, "the irons were tied with one-half inch rope with two double hitches. Only his hip and back were exposed."

"You couldn't tell who he was, his face was so eaten by the crabs," added John Beadle.

A friend of LeBoeuf, Charles Burgers, who had viewed the body, testified that he was sure it was that of James LeBoeuf, who had been missing since he left work the afternoon of July 1. Burgers said he recognized the clothes LeBoeuf had been wearing, and particularly noted the odd shaped and proportioned thumb. "I'd know those thumbs anywhere," Burgers declared.

Burgers, B. Mule, Jr., Jarod Y. Garber, and Bennie R. Mule signed the coroner's report "that the deceased came to his death as the result of two gunshot wounds on the left side, one just below the heart, penetrating the body and making their exit just below the axilla on the right side, said wounds having been made with a weapon in the hands of a party or parties unknown, after which the body was placed in Lake Palourde, the place and time of death being unknown."

Augmenting the jury's report, Dr. Horton added, "To the right of the abdomen was what appeared to be an exit of a gunshot wound which entered the left side just below the heart. In the chest region of the heart there was another point of entry of some kind of bullet apparently exiting the right side. The abdomen had been cut apparently with a sharp instrument in the middle line and entire distance from the forson cartilage to the symphisis pulis and the abdomen was cut at right angles to the first cut on the left side. A pocket watch and $1.25 in silver money was found in the pockets of the dead man."

Sheriff Pecot had sought out Police Chief Blakeman and Walter T. Gilmore, an assistant district attorney who had been working with Blakeman since the body was found. Gilmore's office was located on the second floor of the Bank of Morgan City on Frerett Street, just off Front Street. The office was reached by a steep staircase.

"Who do you have lined up for questioning?" were the first wheezing words out of Pecot's mouth as he topped the stairs. The sheriff, unaccustomed to much physical exertion, was breathing hard.

"I'd say bring in the victim's widow," Blakeman said. "She never reported LeBoeuf missing. She's my sister-in-law, you know. I married her sister. Her name is Ada Bonner LeBoeuf."

It's a starting point," Pecot agreed. "Let's bring her up here."

Meanwhile, marking the gossip around town linking Dr. Dreher with a reported triangle involving LeBoeuf and his wife, and the name of James Beadle (no close relation to the men who found the body) who was Dreher's "Man Friday," Pecot elected to question each separately.

Blakeman was dispatched to bring the widow in. Pecot decided she might be more at ease if a relative—even by marriage—escorted her to be interrogated.

The office was in semi-darkness when the woman arrived, with only light from the lamp on Gilmore's desk. The outside daylight was blotted out by spring-operated roll-up fabric shades, dark green inside and cream colored out, the better to reflect the sun.

When the woman entered the room, Pecot noted she had a certain grace of movement about her. At thirty-eight, Ada was a handsome woman, he observed. She was not of the flapper genre with their bobbed hair and low-waisted hemlines, but a well-proportioned woman, perhaps 5 feet 8 inches tall and approximately 140 pounds. She had high cheekbones in a face grown plump since girlhood, and a high forehead (not necessarily indicating intelligence, Pecot thought). Her jet black marcelled hair was pulled back by the cloche which covered it and held in place with bobby pins.

It was part of Pecot's routine to study the eyes of those he questioned. Ada's were shining and gray, and she had about the whitest teeth he had ever seen which showed when she smiled, and that was often, a small uncertain smile which suggested to him that she was uncomfortable.

Gilmore asked when she had last seen her husband. In response, Ada recounted her story—that her husband was home for supper about 5:30 p.m., that he had suggested the visit to her brother's home and the subsequent boat ride, that during the boat ride they encountered another boat and shots were fired, and she left the scene hurriedly and returned home. And that was about the sum of her answers.

"I docked the boat and went on home. When the kids asked where he was, I told them Jim and I had an argument and he would come back when he cooled off."

"When he didn't come back, I thought maybe he had gone to the district office in Lafayette on business. He often does."

"And what was that argument about?" Gilmore asked.

"Nothing important. In fact I really can't recall what we fussed about. Just one of those little family matters, I suppose," she replied, her voice trailing off, her hands nervously playing with the patent leather purse in her lap.

Still the steady stream of questions came. Ada held to her story, repeating over and again that was all she knew about the matter, and as for that man at the undertakers, that was not Jim.

Then where was Jim?

"In another part of the state," she maintained.

The questioning continued, Blakeman stepped into the hall and shortly thereafter Pecot followed.

"What do you think of the situation?" Pecot asked him.

"I think you have a party in there that could tell you all about it," Blakeman said.

"You don't mean that you think Mrs. LeBoeuf killed her husband!" Pecot said with a start.

"No, I don't think that, but I think she knew all about it."

Pecot returned to the room, and Blakeman went downstairs to a nearby restaurant where he sat drinking coffee. That was the way most Cajuns relaxed. Despite the heat, the coffee seemed to cool them off. A short time later, leaving Ada with Gilmore, Pecot came down for lunch and joined him.

"How you making out?" Blakeman asked.

"I am not getting much," Pecot answered. "She seems to be pretty hard. She won't say anything. Will you come back with me and see if you can help?" Pecot asked Blakeman. "Maybe she will tell you. After all, you're her brother-in-law."

Back in Gilmore's office, Blakeman started talking to Ada in a slow and soothing voice about the killing. "Sis, it will be better if you turn state's evidence. Better tell what you know. We know a lot more than you think. I would advise you to tell what you know. In cases I've heard of when there was more than one person implicated in a murder, and one turned state's evidence and told all he knew, it helped him out and it was easier for him."

Not only was Ada confused, she was tired. She had spent the better part of the day being drilled. She had longed for a friendly face, someone to advise her what to do. An attorney, perhaps, but no one had suggested that.

Blakeman cajoled, "If you tell us I'll do everything I legally can to help you."

The offer seemed to thaw Ada's denials, and she related that she and Jim had taken two boats "because one was too small. . . . We stayed there [at Emory's, her brother] for a little while, until about 7:30, then we went for a boat ride. We met another boat and I heard two shots fired. In the excitement I just turned my boat around and came on back. My brother asked me where my husband was, and I just said he was at the corner waiting for me."

Over and over, her interrogators asked "Who was it that killed Jim?"

"I don't know," she said time and again.

"You were only eight to ten feet away and did not recognize them?"

Ada stopped and thought back. In her mind's eye she saw the half light of a mid-summer evening, that time when day reluctantly accepts the sovereignty of night.

"No, it was too dark," she slowly answered.

"Did Doc shoot him?"

"No."

"How do you know it wasn't Doc shot him if it was so dark you couldn't see who it was?"

"The man that shot him was a smaller man than Dr. Dreher."

The questions went on some three hours while Pecot paced the floor, shooting questions at the woman while Gilmore just listened.

Ada persisted that the body retrieved from the lake was not that of her husband.

"You don't have to worry about that. It certainly is Jim's body," Blakeman assured her.

"None of the boys saw him," she rejoined.

"Well, Sis, I was practically the cause of them not seeing him. Those boys wanted to go and see him. I advised them not to go. I said, 'You boys, the last time you saw your father he was well and hearty and you will always remember him that way. He is a horrible, horrible sight!'"

Ada persisted in her denials. Blakeman saw the expression on her face and knew she was near a breaking point. She seemed to be evaluating what had been said. Finally, in a torrent of words, but with no show of emotion she spoke.

"I am sorry. I have lied to you and Mr. Pecot. I have lied to my people. I have lied to everybody. I am going to tell you the truth."

Ada then falteringly outlined the story. It all began weeks back, she said, when her husband received an anonymous tip from a woman "across the tracks" accusing her of having an affair with Dr. Dreher. The doctor had been a family friend—that is all—for a number of years, she said, but after the note Jim had become more and more jealous of her, and abusive physically, as well.

She said she lured LeBoeuf to the lake with a note from Dr. Dreher that he would be on the lake that night and wanted to patch things up. She said she paddled one small boat following her husband until they were near the "colored schoolhouse" and she was present when she heard Dr. Dreher call out.

"Is that you Jim?"

"Yes. Who is that?"

"This is Doc. I received a note from your wife this afternoon saying that you would meet me on friendly terms."

"Friendly, hell," and LeBoeuf cursed. "You have that damned fellow Beadle with you." Ada said her husband fired into the dark. "Friends be damned. Didn't I tell you if you ever spoke to me or my wife I would kill you?"

Ada now said her husband fired first and that Beadle was the one who shot him. She paddled to the shore, saw and heard nothing more and hurried home, she added.

"On Saturday afternoon, the day after the killing, Mrs. Rosalie Hebert, wife of Noah Hebert, brought me a note from Dr. Dreher in which the doctor sympathized with me for all the trouble I was in. I had my car and I had gone for a ride and saw Dr. Dreher's car; he never stopped me but I stopped him. It was there that I told him that Jim was gone. I told him that I did not tell anyone that Jim had been shot because, if I did, they would put two and two together and might accuse him. 'Well, kid, that is just about what it would be.' This meeting was on Federal Avenue at about 8 o'clock."

Ada did not go home after the session in Gilmore's office. Blakeman said he would get his wife, Ada's sister, to gather any personal things she might need and take them to the jail in Franklin. Emory Bonner and his wife would take the kids and watch over them, Blakeman assured his sister-in-law.

Once they reached the jail in Franklin, Ada sat down with a stenographer and haltingly dictated a confession, weighing every word, frequently asking "Must I go on?" and told that she must, she repeated much of what she had said already, although some details were at variance:

"On our way to my sister-in-law's, my husband stopped and took a boat, I don't know whose boat, and we went out to my sister-in-law's home.

We stayed there a little while, until about 7:30 p.m. Then we went for a boat ride on which we met another boat, and I heard two shots fired. In my excitement, I just turned my boat around and came on back. My brother asked me where my husband was and I just said that he was at the corner waiting for me, so I went on home and never said anything about it to anyone. So the next morning the girl [Liberty] asked where Jim was, and I said "Jim has left town." That was all I said.

"While I never heard Dr. Dreher threaten my husband's life, my husband threatened Dr. Dreher's many times. He even tried to get him to come to the house and had his rifle in the parlor. I don't know whether he was going to use it, but still you can never tell."

By this time, Ada was rambling, not knowing she had covered the same ground and, lost, was going in circles.

"They were just about eight to ten feet away when the shots were fired. I was back of Jim's boat and when the two shots were fired, I turned and started home. The boat rocked a little bit but did not turn over. I did not know whether the boat Jim was in turned over."

After giving her statement, Ada admitted that she knew Dr. Dreher was present at the scene of the shooting. She did not know, she insisted, who fired the gun.

The night of the confession was the first of many Ada was to spend in the jail for months to follow. She was placed in a third floor cell, specifically designed for those accused of murder. It overlooked the gallows.

4

The large two-story home was marked by a steep roof and a wide outcropping segment with striped canvas awning matching that which protected the entire front first floor gallery. Sheriff Pecot stood at the gate in the neat picket fence which surrounded the yard. He was impressed, but he did not show it. Followed by Deputy W. J. Blunt, he strode to the heavy etched glass front door, noting the gold lettering on it: "Thomas E. Dreher, M. D."

Dr. Dreher opened the door. He was a man about six feet tall, large but well proportioned, almost athletic, and about 175 pounds, the product of a strict regime of diet and exercise. He had an almost indiscernible twitch on the left side of his face, the result of a minor stroke some years earlier.

Pecot estimated that he was about 48 years old. He had brown hair in which a touch of distinguishing gray showed at the temples.

"Dr. Dreher? I am Sheriff Charles Pecot. I have a warrant to arrest you."

"I have been expecting it all evening. I knew you were coming to get me," said Dreher, his voice quivering and unsteady. "This is hell. I have been in hell."

He led the way, with Pecot following, into a tastefully furnished living room, reflecting the preferences, the sheriff assumed, of Dreher's wife. Though it still bore traces of late Victorianism—lots of potted fern, the tall vases either side of the fireplace with its large framed beveled mirror—it boasted a large oversized couch and matching armchairs with an abundance of needlepoint pillows.

Dreher continued a kind of rambling and disjointed soliloquy which required no question.

"That man has threatened my life so often that I have been in fear at all times that he would take a shot at me. I have kept my home in darkness for fear he would take a shot at me through the windows at night."

As he spoke, a petite, dignified and refined woman came into the room, together with two younger women. They all had inquisitive expressions.

"This is Sheriff Pecot. He has some questions to ask me, and I think it will be better if we do it in my room," the doctor said.

He led the sheriff and his deputy down a hall to a darkened bedroom where he sat on the edge of a bed, gripping the mattress with his hands until his knuckles were white.

"I did not do the killing. I told Jim Beadle that he would kill me before the end of the week, and Jim Beadle said to me, 'You bring that'—and he used a cuss word—'out somewhere and I will put him away where he will never bother you or anyone else again as long as you live!'"

Dreher stopped momentarily. He withdrew a large white linen handkerchief from his hip pocket and mopped at his brow and face before he continued.

"I did not kill Jim LeBoeuf. James Beadle killed him. But he did it all for me, and I am just as guilty as he is."

He stopped again and stood up, wringing his hands. "Oh why didn't I do what I started to do? I started to shoot my head off, but I waited too late!"

He sat on the bed again and began running his hand under the mattress, but Pecot grabbed his arm on one side while Deputy Blunt restrained him on the other. Blunt removed Dreher's hand from beneath the mattress. He was grasping a pistol.

"I was going to give it to my wife," he explained. Later, the two law enforcement officers were to say they thought he meant to take his life.

The sheriff decided that he had Dreher where he wanted him—whipped, defeated, ashamed. It was now time to give him a brief moment, then concentrate on the story the man would tell. The two men sat in silence briefly, only the whirring of an oscillating table fan breaking the quiet. Deputy Blunt stood attentively off to the side.

"How in the world did that woman confess?" Dreher asked of no one in particular, staring off into nothingness. "She wrote me last night she would not tell anybody."

"Start with Friday before July Fourth," Sheriff Pecot prompted. "Tell me what you know."

Dreher brushed his hand across his eyes and began.

"Mrs. LeBoeuf wrote me a note which Liberty delivered to me at my office. She said she and her husband were going on a boat ride near the colored schoolhouse about 8 p. m., 'and you had better get him then or he will get you'—something to that effect."

Dreher continued that he went to get Jim Beadle and the two set out in a green pirogue Beadle owned. He said the LeBoeufs happened along and they met near the school . . . and Beadle shot and killed LeBoeuf.

"We tied LeBoeuf's boat behind ours and towed him out," the doctor said.

"Who put on the weights?" Pecot asked.

"We did."

"Who cut him open? Did you make the incisions?"

"I did not. Beadle is an expert enough hunter and had long experience in cutting up deer and other game after he had killed them. Beadle did it. Beadle did it for me, and I turned my head. I am just as guilty as he is."

"Did you tell him to do it?"

"No, it was his own idea."

"Whose gun did Beadle use?"

"My own, I had given it to Beadle just before we left for the scene."

"What happened to LeBoeuf's boat?"

"Beadle took it and destroyed it . . . broke it up."

"Where was Mrs. LeBoeuf during all of this?"

Dr. Dreher said she was present for the whole thing, had seen Beadle shoot her husband, and did not leave the area until the mutilated body of her husband was dumped into the lake. How could he know at the time that his story was at variance in this regard with Ada's version?

Despite repeated questions, Dreher would only reiterate his answers or declare he could not recall. Pecot saw the time had come to disengage and take Dreher into custody. Questioning could continue once he lodged Dreher in jail in Franklin.

"I'm going to have to take him in," Pecot told Mrs. Dreher and daughters Polly and Dorothy. Polly was an adolescent, 15; Dorothy a young woman of 19. Son Ted had not yet arrived home from New Orleans where he was a student at Tulane University. Mrs. Dreher and the girls burst into tears as Pecot had expected.

Quietly and politely, the sheriff suggested that Mrs. Dreher and the girls might gather clothes and other necessities the doctor might need for his stay—"Not too much. You can send whatever more he might need later."

The three men sat silently in the parlor while the doctor's family assembled the things for him to take.

"Mind if I smoke?" the sheriff asked Dreher courteously.

"Go ahead, I don't indulge."

Blunt fidgeted in the quietness, a little uneasy in his surroundings.

The women returned, and Blunt took the valise Dorothy held. As they started out the door, Dreher turned and took his wife into his arms. Both were crying. "I won't be long," he tried to comfort her. "I did not do it."

He turned, and with Pecot holding on to his right arm, Blunt following, haltingly went down his front sidewalk for the last time to the waiting car as his family watched from the porch.

District Attorney Emile Vuillemot, like the other parish officials, lived in Franklin, but had come to Morgan City as soon as he was notified of the body found in the lake. He joined them on the return that night accompanying the sheriff and the prisoner back to the parish seat.

Dr. Dreher seemed nervous, apprehensive. He leaned back in the rear seat of the big car as it approached the ferry landing, having already asked that the curtains be drawn around the rear of the car. A curious crowd had assembled at the ferry landing, trying to peer in at him. The doctor seemed fearful that someone in the crowd might shoot him.

"Can't we speed things up and get aboard?" he pleaded. After the car was on the ferry, Pecot went to the captain and asked that the boat leave ahead of schedule. Once the ferry was underway, Dreher seemed to relax and regain his composure.

"I presume you're enjoying this ride?" Dreher asked the district attorney, his words carrying a note of sarcasm.

"I always feel sorry for those who are in trouble," Vuillemot answered.

"It might be a long time before I enjoy another automobile ride," Dreher said. "You know, I tried to kill myself several times. I should have done it before I got myself into this mess." His thoughts still meandering, he continued, "Of course I didn't kill Jim LeBoeuf."

"Who did?" asked Vuillemot, who was not attempting to question Dreher, but was an eager listener.

"Jim Beadle. It was my double-barrel shotgun that Beadle used and you can find it at my home in Morgan City."

"How much did you give him?"

"I didn't give him one cent for his work. He did it purely on account of the great friendship he has for me."

With this, Dreher offered no more information except to say that LeBoeuf had been killed "back of the colored schoolhouse" and then towed in his own boat into the lake.

The doctor fell silent again as if musing on his problems. The heavy four-door green Buick seemed to hurtle forward in the blackness with Deputy Blunt at the wheel, his thick neck and broad shoulders straining as he held tight to the steering wheel, guiding the car through the wet gravel, avoiding the water that sometimes still overflowed the Teche and stood treacherously close to the road's edge. The barrel-chested lawman was familiar with the road, but leery of any erosion, and he sometimes found the mound of gravel pushed to the center of the road by two-way traffic an extra hazard which, if hit at excessive speed, could divert the direction of the front wheels and spin the car out of control.

In the uncertain yellow glare of the car's headlights Dreher imagined apparitions, gray, spectral, among the fibrous streamers cascading from the centuries-old live oaks on either side of the road, but he realized it was only a canopy of Spanish moss. He had the sense of time long gone, never to return, and yet there it was. Time was real, and despite the dreamlike events, he was here, shivering in the back seat, his wrists manacled before him.

A few miles from Berwick, rounding a large curve, Blunt slowed his speed to accommodate the little town of Patterson, largely a sawmill hamlet. The several general stores, a pharmacy and bank, plus an assortment of small businesses lined either side of the sparsely lighted roadway. The general stores were still open, their interiors dimly lit by naked light bulbs snaking down from exposed wiring to outline late shoppers, mostly Negroes, field hands from nearby plantations.

Further down the street on the bayou side, near the outskirts of town, the doctor recognized the big two-story residence which he had heard Dr. Clarence Aycock intended to refurbish as a hospital for his private practice.

Now the lights were fewer, most to the bayou side where sugarcane workers occupied old slave quarters, and where occasional coal oil lamps and their blackened glass chimneys gave off eerie shadows from the interior of the cabins.

Beyond that, on the left they passed the Harry P. Williams airport where airmen tinkered with developing swift planes for sport and commerce. Off to the right, at the bayou's edge, was the hunting lodge at which Williams and his silent screen actress-wife, Marguerite Clark, entertained when they were not in residence at their lavish St. Charles Avenue home in New Orleans.

They hardly slowed at Calumet where the road curved sharply past the general store. They passed the little community of Centerville in complete darkness and soon approached Garden City, almost the outskirts of Franklin.

Finally the car entered an arcade of stately oaks, arching the roadway, interspersed with dimly lighted street standards. Along either side of the road stood several imposing antebellum homes.

They came to a stop as the road dead-ended and jogged around the town square, site of the St. Mary Parish Courthouse and their destination, the adjacent jail.

Ada LeBoeuf was already in residence, and Sheriff Pecot, even then, had his men seeking out the third principal, James Beadle.

5

Earlier, Sheriff Pecot dispatched deputies to the home of James Beadle just outside Morgan City's corporate limits. It was an inauspicious dwelling as one would expect of a wife and seven children and a father with no steady income.

The drab, unpainted frame house was undistinguished from many others found along the bayous—a porch across the front, its windows protected by wooden shutters of solid planking buttressed by criss-crossing smaller wood supports, admitting no light when closed.

Beadle, "a rough type of man" as characterized by news stories of the case, was 45 years old and only about 5 feet 7 inches tall with short, straggly black hair and a matching bristle of a mustache. His flashing black eyes had a tendency to smolder when his dander was up. His sun-leathered skin was almost bronze, and though uneducated in terms of books, he was well versed in ways of the swamp. Beadle claimed to be a hunting and fishing guide, but most people in Morgan City were aware that Dr. Dreher was his real source of income. The doctor was widely known to be the benefactor of many down-on-their-luck residents, even to the point of paying medical expenses out of his own pocket. Just until the recipients were able to repay it, he would say.

The wiry, little Beadle had a sharp temper and a low flash point, although he could reveal a stoic indifference to things which did not involve him or his family.

When the deputies first arrived at his home, Beadle showed that facet of his personality. With his wife and children around him, he steadfastly maintained that on the night in question he was at home with his family. He had nothing to do with the matter. His family did not dispute him. They rarely did and when they did it was at their peril.

The deputies, nonetheless, took him to Franklin for further questioning. They had witnesses who placed him at the scene of the crime. At the jail he was confronted by Dreher.

"I've told everything Jim. Why don't you go on and tell what you know?"

"I don't know what you're talking about." Beadle's face was blank and unrevealing.

"Jim, you might as well tell the whole thing now. The woman has told how it all happened and I have told all I know. Now you ought to tell. The jig is up."

"I don't know anything about that," said Beadle, not looking Dreher in the eye, but his mouth twitching beneath his mustache.

The taciturn trapper did have some words for the deputies. However, they were not about the case.

"Why do I get the smallest cell? The Doc has that big one on the corner of the building. I barely got room to turn around." The lawmen didn't answer him.

It was the small things in life that meant the most to Beadle. Like the favoritism they showed to Dreher. Beadle had to eat prison fare, Dreher had his meals sent in from The Club restaurant. The doctor had preference on getting his hair cut. Little things, maybe, but Beadle felt somehow belittled, and such things could have an impact on the case later on.

Thursday night, the first night in jail, was a long one. Most of it was filled with continuing questions, preparatory to final confessions from Ada and Dr. Dreher.

District Judge James D. Simon, only 28 years old and one of the state's youngest jurists, was to preside over the case. His judicial district included St. Martin, Iberia, and St. Mary parishes. Normally, the court was in recess at this time of the year, but public pressure, generated by horror at the nature of the crime and unsubstantiated charges of illicit relations between Ada and Dr. Dreher, prompted Judge Simon to call for a special session of the St. Mary Grand Jury. That meant that the defendants' confessions would be needed by Tuesday when the jury was to convene.

Thus, early Friday the trio was roused from a near-sleepless night, breakfasted, and hailed before interrogators and shorthand specialists to record their statements for signatures.

Still Beadle was keeping his distance from admitting any part in the murder. "I don't know anything about this killing and I'll say that until I die. If they say that about me, they are telling a lie."

Gory murder details and prospects of a major "sex trial" were attracting national attention. A dispatch printed by the *New York Times* on Sunday read, in part:

> Beadle is the enigma of the case. At first he was regarded as a secondary figure, a mere tool of Dr. Dreher. His attitude of silence in jail has begun to add luster to his name in the Teche country. He alone of the trio has steadfastly refused to admit any complicity in the murder of James J. LeBoeuf.

> A conversation with him today (Saturday) indicated that if he ever confesses it will be a great surprise.
>
> He is the only one of the trio who would consent today to being photographed. It was not in his cell. In accommodating fashion this man who is alleged to have boasted privately that he would 'put LeBoeuf away so he wouldn't bother the doctor anymore' politely asked the photographer to wait until he could don a shirt. He agreeably posed a dozen times.
>
> But when asked if Dr. Dreher and Mrs. LeBoeuf had told the truth, he answered in the negative. Sometimes his attitude is sullen, at times merely phlegmatic. He is never defiant, and interest is beginning to switch from the enamored pair to the little man with a dark red [*sic.*] mustache who says he did not commit the murder, and is insistent in this declaration even when the whole world believes he did.

Sheriff Pecot, meantime, continued to say he felt Beadle would eventually confess his role in the crime.

"I will confront Beadle with two persons from Morgan City who said they saw him cut the murder boat to pieces," Pecot said. He said authorities were holding Beadle's pocketknife, alleged to have been used to cut LeBoeuf open, bearing unidentified red brown stains and the shotgun which supposedly fired the fatal shots.

Dr. Dreher realized the noose was being prepared and so the defendants had to be ready, too. Despite his reputed wealth, he had to mortgage his home for attorneys to represent not only himself, but Ada and Beadle as well. He selected former State Senator James R. Parkerson and L. O. Pecot.(distantly related to the sheriff) both of Franklin.

On Saturday, Pecot announced that a careful watch was being kept on Dr. Dreher to prevent a suicide attempt. The sheriff said that several times in questioning the doctor mentioned he wished he had blown his brains out, and the sheriff recounted the story of the pistol and the mattress at the questioning in his home.

Pecot said he had refused the requests of Dreher and Ada to see one another. The doctor seemed more cheerful and spoke with his wife by telephone. Pecot said Dreher told his wife "You know what to believe and what not to believe. About nine tenths of what you have heard is not true." Dreher was now spending most of his time conferring with his attorneys and his son, Thomas E. Dreher, Jr.

On Saturday, defense attorneys Parkerson and Pecot went to Morgan City to conduct their own investigation and returned to say they were convinced they would be able to free all three of the accused. At the same time, Parkerson denounced some news stories as "false and untrue and deliberate attempts to stir up prejudice against the defendants." He said he referred to headlines purporting to indicate that Dr. Dreher attempted to commit suicide as he was being arrested.

Parkerson asked the mounting contingent of out-of-town newspaper correspondents drawn to the lurid murder to request that the public withhold judgment until the trial. "There is a legitimate defense and I am firmly convinced of my ability to clear all three defendants."

District Attorney Vuillemot answered that he would seek first degree murder indictments against all three defendants when the grand jury met the next day.

When the barber, W. T. Walker, shaved Dreher on Monday, he said the doctor complained he was unable to exercise properly in his cell and sent a request to the sheriff that a sparring partner be sent to work out with him in his cell. Walker said he declined the invitation to spar with Dreher. And the sheriff ignored the request. When Walker went to Beadle and offered to shave him, he said the trapper gave him a cold reception and declined to have his five-day beard trimmed.

As they settled down to prison life, Ada began to receive visitors. One was her aged mother, Mrs. E. C. Bonner, who wept bitterly as she climbed the stairs. Ada's brother, Emory, and several nieces and nephews also visited her. Nearly prostrate with grief, Mrs. Bonner told newsmen as she emerged, "I believe in my daughter. Her only mistake was that she did not at once report what she had seen that awful night."

Newspaper reporters still were barred from the jail, and when a stranger came to his cell door, Dr. Dreher asked his identity and said he hoped that man was not a reporter. "My wife would come to see me today, but she is afraid to show her face. Her picture will appear in the paper if she does," the doctor complained.

The industrious Sheriff Pecot continued to unearth evidence in the case. He announced that he had found the oversize pirogue in which he claimed LeBoeuf was mutilated after his slaying, and that he had found six more unnamed witnesses. Two, he said, could testify they saw Dr. Dreher and Beadle paddle away from Morgan City toward the scene of the killing the night of July 1. Four more, he said would say that they saw Dr. Dreher and Beadle load the green pirogue on the doctor's car.

Pecot indicated that stains on the pirogue, found in Bayou Wax, a tributary of Lake Palourde, resembled blood, and Pecot surmised that LeBoeuf was shot in his own boat then transferred to the pirogue where he was mutilated, weighted, and cast into the lake.

Pecot also questioned Mrs. Noah Hebert, a friend of Mrs. LeBoeuf who often visited the LeBoeuf home, and was one of the few women Leboeuf permitted to visit Ada. She frequently served as a seamstress, making Ada's clothes. While Jim and Ada often appeared ideal mates in public, she said in private Ada showed her bodily bruises which she said Jim inflicted upon her.

Mrs. Hebert saw nothing wrong in carrying notes to and from the Doc and Ada, inasmuch as they had been seen together in public and been objects of public gossip for years. She said Dr. Dreher became attracted to Ada about seven years before.

All day before the grand jury session, Dr. Dreher was in high spirits. When the sheriff asked him about the boat he and Beadle used, he said his attorneys had instructed him not to do any more talking. Changing the conversation, Dreher said, "Let's forget the killing and go out to a moving picture show."

To the barber who came to shave him, the Doc asked, "Please don't scratch me because when I go before the grand jury tomorrow the reporters may see me, and I don't want them to think I tried to commit suicide."

Tuesday, July 12, was pivotal in the LeBoeuf murder as the grand jury met to hear evidence. Judge Simon was prompt. He convened court at 10 a.m. and immediately charged the jury without reference to the case they would be considering. "I have called the court into special session because I believe the public interest demands it and, as grand jurors, of a body forming a component part of the court, I charge you to consider matters which may be brought before you with fairness and impartiality." He instructed the jury in the rules of the court, and informed them that they should return a true bill if it was the opinion of nine of the twelve members that one should be returned.

The state paraded a score of witnesses before the jury. Pecot started them early, hoping to get that part of the trial over quickly. There was no doubt in his mind that the evidence already gathered would merit the death penalty.

District Attorney Vuillemot accompanied the jury into its rooms and called his witnesses one by one. Leading off was Cleveland Beadle (among those who found the body), followed by Alcide Mayon (also in the discovery party), assistant coroner C. C. DeGravelles, Parish Coroner C. M. Horton, Billy Mule, Jr. (who aided in recovery of the body), Charles Burgers (who identified the body), Sheriff Pecot, Louis Ratcliffe (night officer at Morgan City), H. G. Amen (secretary to the coroner), Emory Bonner (Ada's brother whose home she visited the night of the murder), L. B. Blakeman (Morgan City chief of police and Ada's brother-in-law), and W. J. Blunt (the deputy sheriff who went with Sheriff Pecot to Dreher's home to arrest him.)

While the jury heard evidence, the three defendants sat calmly in their cells, Dreher in his large second floor corner cell overlooking Bayou Teche, Beadle in a smaller cell lodged next to black prisoners, and Ada in her third floor cell.

About noon each of them received Bibles, the wrappings bearing a return address of Mrs. W. D. Carroll of New Orleans. Beadle, who had received a minister for prayer in his cell, seemed particularly touched by the gift of a Bible.

During early afternoon, Alex Ratcliffe, Beadle's brother-in-law who lived in Berwick, visited him. Beadle told him, "I am getting along all right, and you can say to the folks I don't need anything. If they hang me, well that is all there will be to it."

Sheriff Pecot visited Beadle after Ratcliffe departed. He predicted to newsmen that the trapper would break down before morning and confess to his role in the killing.

Meanwhile, a new allegation came from James LeBoeuf's aged mother, Mrs. Willie Husband, a matron at the Jesuit school at Franklin. The woman would become a steady flow of venom directed against the accused. Her voice high-pitched, the woman told newsmen she believed there was an attempt to poison her son two years before. Whining, she told her story accentuated by years of converting Cajun into English and back again.

"My son was sick for three whole days before Ada called me. Dr. Dreher, his physician, told me that he was ill from drinking condensed milk in his coffee, but no other member of the family was sick and they had been drinking the same milk. My son was suspicious then and told me he thought he had been poisoned. He would have left his wife then, but I begged him to try to get along for my sake."

Her story was the first of many she would feed to the welcoming newsmen, stories calculated to cast her son as a victim in a loveless marriage, of herself as a long-suffering mother, and the helpless mother-in-law of a faithless woman who cared little for her family.

As the afternoon wore on, the jail courtyard filled with acquaintances of the accused and relatives of LeBoeuf who stood outside the jail hoping to catch a glimpse of the prisoners. Each one seemed to have his own theory about the case, each of them differing from the other.

The doctor's acquaintances painted a picture of him as a respected community leader in Morgan City. A parish official said Dreher once held high office in the Ku Klux Klan and was always active in civic work.

Shortly after 2:30 p.m., Judge Simon convened court to receive the grand jury's report from L. M. Folse, jury foreman, and it was read to the court by Wilbur Kramer, the judge's clerk. The indictments were then turned over to the defendants' attorney, Mr. Parkerson.

Judge Simon set trial for July 25 and arraignment of all three defendants at 10 a.m. on Wednesday, July 13. There was little doubt that justice was being stampeded, and the clamor of the public had started it.

6

Parkerson had instructed his clients beforehand. Arraignment would be the first real impression the public would obtain of them. As such, it could have a major impact on their case. Their appearances and demeanor while in the public eye had to be orchestrated carefully.

Accompanied by Sheriff Pecot enroute from the jail quarters to the courtroom, the doctor turned and shook hands with Beadle, whose arm was gripped by Deputy Sheriff G. B. Pecot. Ada was in the custody of Deputy Sheriff Arthur Martel.

"The sheriff tells me I cannot talk to you, Jim, but I want to shake your hand," said Dreher.

The doctor was less than cordial to newsmen who snapped his picture as he entered the courthouse, but regained his high spirits when he reached the courtroom, smiling to friends along the way. He was attired in a gray summer suit which had not been pressed since he was imprisoned. It bulged at the knees, making him appear shabby, hardly the well-dressed Beau Brummel for which he had the reputation. As he sat in the place the deputy indicated, a newsman, not knowing Dreher's identity, took a seat beside him. "The newspapers are painting me up as a pretty hardened criminal" Dreher said to him. The newsman denied it. Defense Attorney Parkerson objected to Judge Simon that newsmen should refrain from talking with the defendants. Judge Simon ordered the reporter to stop.

Ada was seated several feet to the doctor's rear. She, too, had faced a barrage of cameras enroute to the courtroom, but seemed in good humor as she entered. She was dressed in mourning black satin, stylishly cut, offset by white lace at the throat and cuffs of the long sleeved gown. Her hair was carefully coifed in a series of waves down to the nape of the neck and appeared shorter than in fact it was. Her face was heavily powdered almost mask-like, but she wore no rouge, and only the hint of a dark pink lipstick.

Beadle came in showing little concern about the proceedings. He sat about ten feet from Dreher. The trapper was dressed as in the work-a-day world. Although in his shirt sleeves, his clothes were immaculately clean, his black mohair trousers newly pressed, and his checkered tie neatly tied. Partly covered by a stubby black beard, his face was not without expression.

As soon as the indictment was read, District Attorney Vuillemot entered the motion for arraignment. Parkerson posed an objection, "My clients have not had time to consider arraignment," he said.

"The law does not require any delays in this case," said Judge Simon, his starched white collar and somber dark blue tie showing at the neck of his black robe. Though young, he was striving to present the sterner side of the law. "Objection overruled."

"I now enter a plea of 'not guilty,' for all three accused," Parkerson said.

Vuillemot moved that the trial date be set for July 25.

"Your honor, I object to that motion!" retorted Parkerson. "I object on the ground that this will not allow the accused sufficient time to prepare for their defense. I understand that the court already has issued an order for the jury commission to call veniremen for that date and I would like to move that the court rescind that order."

Again Judge Simon overruled the objection and ordered the trial be set for July 25.

All the time the formal indictment was being read, Ada stood facing the bench, her head held high, looking neither right nor left. She appeared almost defiant. Twice she pressed a handkerchief to her nose, but her eyes showed no sign of tears.

To her right stood Dr. Dreher who was also clasping a handkerchief, nervously twisting it while he kept his eyes straight ahead. Next to him, Beadle appeared more concerned, but looked around the courtroom and down at his feet, still listening attentively.

Ada and the Doc were allowed a brief moment together before being returned to their cells.

"Don't break down, Ada, keep your nerves together," he said as they parted.

"All right, Doc. You can depend on me," Ada replied.

The steps of all three suggested dejection as they headed back to their cells.

"I want to be out in the fresh air," complained Ada to Deputy Martel, the jailer.

As she descended the courthouse steps, Ada encountered a photographer. "You move fast, Big Boy, and you are using your head. If you don't get my picture now I don't know when you will get one. This is your best chance."

In front of the jail as they headed in were Beadle's wife and children. Pleasant Beadle, ten years old and youngest son, told newsmen, "Papa's in trouble and we had to come and see him." Irene Beadle, twenty years old and the only daughter, walked with her mother, Alice Lovell Beadle. Irene said her father was lonely and had written asking someone come to see him. "All of us had to come when we got the letter," she said.

Mrs. Dreher did not come, instead staying at her Morgan City home with her two daughters, son, and a nephew. Although she spoke of her family's "great blow," she declined to see any but her friends. Through them she declared she forgave her husband for everything.

Overnight, Parkerson and L. O. Pecot, his associate, decided upon their first weapon of defense, an assault on the composition of the prospective jury. In a letter to the jury commission, the attorneys challenged impaneling of the trial jury. They argued that the Louisiana statute relative to women serving on juries conflicted with the Fourteenth and Nineteenth Amendments to the U. S. Constitution. State law provided that in order to serve on a jury, first women had to ask that their names be included among those from whom juries were to be selected, the idea being that this was a way to protect women from having to serve on juries which would hear distasteful trial subject matter.

No woman had requested to be included in jury venires, the jury commission confirmed. Parkerson said this was a discrimination against women. The provision that women make declaration of willingness to serve was unconstitutional.

But Judge Simon ordered the jury commission to proceed with furnishing the names of thirty citizens from which a jury may be selected. If Parkerson's objection were upheld it would mean that the fate of the three accused might be settled in federal rather than state court.

On Thursday, July 14, Mrs. Willie Husband, grieving mother of Jim LeBoeuf, went to the courthouse and offered her assistance to Sheriff Pecot in the prosecution of the alleged murderers of the son who she saw buried only a week before. Mrs. Husband offered her small savings to Pecot to retain attorneys to help the prosecution, but the offer was declined.

"Jim was a good boy and I want to do everything I can to keep those people in jail," she said. "If what little help I can give will do anything I want you to accept it." She projected a humble matron at the Jesuit school on Franklin's outskirts, and wore her work apron, using the corners to dry tears coursing down her cheeks. She said she did not want to see anyone hanged. "All I want is to keep whoever killed my boy in jail so they can't hurt anybody like they have hurt me."

Jim always had been good to her, Mrs. Husband said. "He was too good to his wife or all this would not have happened. It is mighty hard keeping on with my cooking and sewing and cleaning when I have to stop ever so often to think about my dear boy."

Tears continued down her cheeks as she said, "I could not have gone to take flowers to my boy if I had not offered my help in punishing those people that killed him. The sheriff says the state will handle them all right, so I guess I have done all I can."

Jailers reported the first words from Dreher each morning were "How is Ada? How is Ada, Mr. Sheriff? I hope she is all right, and I would like mighty well to have a long talk with her." The couple were given little opportunity for conversation since they were jailed. In his cell after the brief walk from the courthouse, Doc's thoughts again were of Ada. He spoke of her to his jailers and said he was glad she was holding up under the strain.

After all of the sheriff's public comments that he felt Beadle would confess, the wily little trapper was maintaining his silence. Pecot seemed resigned to the fact Beadle would not talk, but he was also confident that evidence so far gathered was sufficient to gain convictions, possibly the death penalty. Ada's own confession should be enough in itself, he thought.

Even now, New Iberia identification expert Compton J. Labauve was pouring over dim outlines of three fingerprints taken from the oversized pirogue in which Dr. Dreher and Beadle were seen riding the night of the killing. The prints were taken from the port side of the pirogue near the bow. They would be compared with fingerprints of Beadle and the Doc taken at the jail. If the fingerprints matched those of LeBoeuf, the state might continue its plans to prosecute Beadle for the murder. If they were those of Dreher, plans would have to be changed.

Authorities noted that Dreher, when arrested, admitted being present in the boat when LeBoeuf was killed, but said Beadle did the shooting. The state accepted that story, but if Beadle was rowing the boat at the time, prosecutors said, it would have been virtually impossible for him to have done the shooting since the position of the oarsman would have prevented his having within reach the shotgun with which LeBoeuf was killed.

Prosecutors said that if fingerprints showed Dreher was sitting forward in the craft, not standing at the oars, he might be charged with the actual shooting for which he blamed Beadle. Investigators expressed doubt of Dreher's story that Beadle did the killing, but were unable to establish a motive which the doctor might have had for laying the blame on his old friend, especially when the doctor admitted the killing was done out of Beadle's friendship and at the instigation of both him and Ada.

Friday came, and Walker, the barber, arrived to shave Dreher. The Doc was unhappy, Walker said, because he had not been shaved Thursday. He said the Doc did not speak of the murder case, but of his longing for the great outdoors and exercise.

From his cell, the Doc said, he could see the placid Teche and see trout and perch as they broke the surface of the water. "When I see those fish jump," he said, "I want to get out and get my reel and go fishing."

On this visit, Walker found Beadle more amenable to him and allowed him to shave him for the first time since he was arrested. Before his stubby beard was removed, Beadle said he felt embarrassed when visitors came to his cell. "Now I can face the women folks who come to see me," he said.

Up on the third floor, Ada wore a stylish dress of white organdy as she entertained friends. Several visitors to whom she had complained of the heat prior to a heavy afternoon rain suggested she have her long black hair bobbed.

"No indeed," she replied. "Bobbed hair is becoming for some women, but I don't' think I would like it. I never had my hair cut, and I don't suppose I ever will."

A flaw to the state's case had come on Thursday when Parkerson pointed out a misspelling of Dr. Dreher's name in the indictment: "Drehr" rather that "Dreher." Action to amend the discrepancy must precede the trial, Parkerson had explained.

District Attorney Vuillemot moved on Saturday (July 16) to insert the letter "e" between the "h" and the "r" in Dreher's name as spelled in the indictment. Judge Simon ordered the defendants and their counsel to court to hear the motion, but Sheriff Pecot said Parkerson was in Morgan City and unable to appear. The judge ordered that the amendment motion be heard the following Monday at 2 p.m. Representatives of the state foresaw no problem in amending the indictment, but wanted it done before the trial in order to prevent any defense effort to quash the indictment.

Jailers reported that the Doc was extremely nervous during Saturday, but Ada was in high spirits. Beadle focused his attention on a letter he received from a self-styled psychic in New Orleans offering to aid him for $50. The psychic claimed he could save Beadle and tell all about the case. Beadle said he had no money. Pecot took the letter.

Elsewhere, the fingerprint expert declared the prints found on the pirogue were too dim and probably could not be used as evidence. Neither could he obtain prints from the gun believed to have been used in the murder.

The *New Orleans Times-Picayune* reported, in part:

> Franklin, eagerly looking forward to the trial, is quiet, but the murder case is still the subject of conversation at almost every dinner table and on every street corner.
>
> On account of the prominence of the principals in the case, older Morgan City residents do not discuss the matter with strangers.
>
> Morgan City's younger generation is different. Viewing the case in typical flaming youth fashion, young people joke even with strangers about the affair. A Morgan City youth said today he is writing a seven-verse song to be titled 'Boat Riding Mama, don't you try to angle-iron me.'

References to 'dangers of pirogue riding' are common in expressions of Morgan City youths.

Sunday was a special day for the defendants. For the first time since their imprisonment, they were allowed to talk confidentially to each other and to confer with their attorneys about the trial to begin a week away.

Monday came, and again the defendants were taken from their jail cells to the courtroom. Although the attorneys hassled over the amendment of the faulty indictment, the spelling of Dreher's name was corrected. Vuillemot dotted all the "i's" and crossed the "t's" this time, saying the accused would have to be arraigned again, and despite the protestations of Parkerson, Judge Simon agreed.

All this occurred as the three defendants sat apparently unconcerned. Ada was less somberly dressed than she was for her first appearance in court. She wore a white organdy dress, with brown collar and a broad brown belt. She looked straight ahead and appeared unconcerned. The Doc seemed more neatly dressed than on his previous visit, but his trousers still were unpressed. Beadle smiled and nodded at friends when he came in, appearing to be not the least worried. Unlike his last visit to the courtroom in his shirt sleeves, the trapper now wore a neat blue coat over his black trousers.

As the defendants prepared to return to their cells, their attorney asked Judge Simon to prevent the press from "harassing" his clients, and Simon ordered their police escorts to protect them from being bothered. But, as they were leaving the courthouse, the Doc grinning sheepishly, pulled Deputy Martel with him as he ducked behind a bush when photographers tried to take his picture. Ada, running the gauntlet of newsmen, giggled and covered her face with a handkerchief. James Beadle seemed to relish the attention. He smiled accommodatingly for photographers. As he was about to enter the jail, he asked his escort to hesitate a moment while a photographer adjusted his camera.

"Jim Beadle's not ashamed to have his picture in the papers," he asserted, "because Jim Beadle knows he hasn't done anything. You won't find me putting a handkerchief over my head. I will try to help you boys because I know you have got orders to get my picture and I know you haven't got anything against me."

Beadle might have been uneducated, but his way with the press would have shamed many a public-relations man. Nor were his actions lost on the public. As Beadle disappeared into the jail, a woman bystander observed," I don't see how that poor man could be guilty. He was entirely different from that brazen woman and he wasn't worried like Dr. Dreher."

Inside the jail, Beadle shook hands with the prosecutors and nodded smilingly at the deputies. Ada and Dr. Dreher were prevented from anything more than salutations before being returned to their cells.

Sheriff Pecot left for New Orleans after the hearing, taking Beadle's knife with him to obtain a chemical analysis of rust colored stains found on it. Beadle said those were not blood stains, but resulted from using the knife to cut a pineapple. The city chemist said the stains appeared to be blood stains, but an examination would require forty days, and he would be unable to testify on the matter when the case went to trial July 25. Sheriff Pecot did not appear disappointed. He said he had enough evidence without the knife to convict the accused. "We've got an airtight case," he said, boarding the train to return to Franklin.

7

It was Saturday, July 23, and workers were hurriedly completing installation of telegraph lines in courthouse offices for the use of newsmen as Judge Simon had permitted.

The courtroom, itself, was reached by climbing the front stairs leading to the second floor level, culminating in a short corridor opening into the chamber. It was a circular room with a metal rail enclosing the judicial bench and court attaches, witness stand, tables for the opposing counsel, seating for the accused and immediate families.

Columns supported the ceiling at intervals in the guard rail, and the rich deep brown of the furniture and woodwork were in sharp contrast to the clean white walls. There was an air of dignity as befits judicial decorum, almost the feeling one might have had in a larger Roman senate of another era.

Judge Simon had assured reporters he would reserve seating for them, but not allow cameras or typewriters. Sheriff Pecot had ordered a long table be placed toward the front of the courtroom for the two dozen or more reporters covering the trial. Capacity of the small courtroom was 300, Simon estimated, including the balcony. He had told Pecot that no more than that number be admitted at a time into the courtroom, and he expressed concern as how to handle the crowd.

Some newspaper reports estimated that as many as 5,000 visitors would be in town for the trial, and that would exceed the population of Franklin, estimated to be 3,200. By late Saturday, however, the vast crowd expectation had not been realized, even though hotels were booked to overflowing, and restaurants were geared for the onslaught of out-of-town newsmen and the "just curious."

Big city newsmen described the courthouse as small. Perhaps it was small by their standards, but it was built as the hub of a small town and from its position in the community, it was large. Its two floors with high ceilings appeared imposing by virtue of four columns at the courthouse entrance, and the dome surmounting the tan brick building. Large, dimly illuminated clocks faced the front, back, and two sides of the dome, marking the time of day and night.

The north (or back) side of the dome faced Bayou Teche, and across the bayou, was a largely uninhabited area. Thus, that clock face served no real purpose except to mark time for the sugarcane field workers, but the architect had argued that the building would be out of proportion and esthetically imperfect if the fourth clock was omitted.

At ground level, to the front of the courthouse, its back to the courthouse stood the obligatory statue of a lone Confederate soldier on a stone pedestal, a replica of sentries standing before countless Southern courthouses. The sentry overlooked a gravel street and the Commercial Bank, a red brick cubicle at the corner of Willow Street. Across Willow Street from the bank, in mid-block, was the town's main barber shop, a focal point for dissemination of gossip on whatever was the menu of the moment, now, of course, the LeBoèuf murder.

On the east side of the courthouse stood a three-story jail, small by contrast to the courthouse, and notable largely for its ugly, dried-blood-red brick, covered with a creepy vegetation newsmen described as ivy, actually a vine known as Virginia Creeper. It served, at least, to soften the harshness of the jail's exterior. Between the courthouse and jail was a courtyard through which one entered the side entrance to the jail, and through which prisoners were escorted to and from their appearances in court.

In small-town fashion the two buildings were located on a square in the middle of town. Unlike most courthouse squares, perhaps because of the paucity of solid ground, it was not a true square. It was approached from the west by U. S. Highway 90, the same highway as approached it from the east. But as the two highway segments met the center of opposite sides of the square, drivers were forced to make a sharp turn and circle half of the square. The other streets which would have constituted a true square were, in reality, not streets at all, but essentially little traveled alleyways, one of which closely edged the bayou to the rear of both courthouse and jail.

Tall royal palms, like those then on the neutral ground of Canal Street in New Orleans, were spaced around the square, but rather than providing an urban air to the town, they served only to accentuate a semi-tropical ambiance.

Since daybreak, one-horse buggies had streamed into town, the weekly "come to town" shopping for groceries, as much a social event as a necessity. The single seat of the conveyance was sheltered by a cab sheathed with black, tarred canvas, and to the rear of the hood was a flat open shelf, much like the rumble seat of an automobile coupe, ideal for carrying bags and boxes, even three or four small children. Locally, the buggies derisively were called "Cajun Cadillacs." It was normal to see them drawn up in front of stores, along the street, wherever could be found a hitching post, and Sunday tethered around the churches.

The vehicles brought husbands, wives, and usually several children, with the women and children dispersing to stores selling piece goods and notions, the men congregating in clusters to discuss the latest. This Saturday, many of them, clad in lightweight denim shirts and often-laundered overalls, convened around the jail. Most of them wore high-topped work shoes and a broad-brimmed coarse straw hat to shield their weather-wrinkled faces from the sun.

Mingling among the locals were reporters from New Orleans and elsewhere. It was a shared experience, the newsmen milking the locals for any tidbit of information about the defendants, the curious seeking anything of interest from the working press, items with which they later could revel their neighbors.

On Sundays, Franklin was a bustling community as churchgoers exited the Church of the Assumption of the Blessed Virgin at the opposite end of Main Street from the courthouse. Outside of the courthouse, it was the largest building in town, and the two structures were only about five blocks apart. Between lay the business district, dry goods stores, Foster's Drug Store (a town gathering spot because of its soda fountain) behind which Dr. Horton maintained his offices for private practice, and the two-story frame Opera House, a rather grand name for the town's silent cinema.

At the westward end of the business district was the Commercial Hotel with its spacious verandah stretching the width of its facade facing Main Street, and which served savory if not gourmet fare in its dining room. Its rooms had been booked solidly a week before, and newsmen lolled on the long porch overlooking the passing parade.

News accounts that day noted the addition of a new attorney to the defense team who arrived by train late Saturday in time for a last minute conference with his fellow legal counsel and the defendants. He was R. F. Walker, a former speaker of the Louisiana House of Representatives. Walker had been Dr. Dreher's roommate when both had been students at Tulane University. That brought the defense team to three.

Dr. Dreher was reported in good spirits the eve of the trial. In a conciliatory mood, he said the press had taken it easy on him the past few days. He visited with family and friends, but declined to talk to reporters. He commented: "Enough has been written about me already."

Down the hall, Beadle asked that a barber be allowed to cut his hair before the trial began. He complained to reporters: "I want to see my picture in the papers. I ain't seen my picture in the papers a single time and they say its been in all of them. How do I know whether it looks like me or not? They brought me a New Orleans paper this morning, but they were pretty careful to see it didn't have any picture of me in it."

He wheedled to reporters, "Can't some of you ladies and gentlemen that works on the papers get me one with my picture in it?" Assured that they would, he grinned. "Thank you very kindly. You know, people sure have been nice to me. I have had plenty of company. My sister and brother-in-law from up the country were passing through this morning and they came in. And there's been lots of strangers, too—strange ladies, ladies I never saw before in all my life, all of them come in and says they hopes I'm feeling well. It helps to pass the time. I sure am glad the trial starts tomorrow. It's been tiresome waiting."

"Are you going to speak for yourself [in the trial]?" asked a reporter.

"You bet I am! And you just bets that when I gets through talking there's going to be some of them state's witnesses that'll wish the floor would just open up and swallow them and the floor ain't gonna do it. Some of them will be doing just like this—" and Beadle began to chew the ends of his thumbs dramatically. "They sure gonna feel sore!"

Up on the third floor, Ada visited with family—her mother; a couple of Misses Blakeman, her nieces, and Joe LeBoeuf, her son. The younger women wore bright Sunday finery, but Mrs. Bonner, Ada's mother, was dressed in a plain black and white checked "bungalow apron." As the party left, Mrs. Bonner called over her shoulder, "Now be good, Ada, but don't be too good. That's been the trouble with you all your life. You've been too good for your own good." She said nothing to newsmen.

"I don't think my grandmother has anything to say to you," said one of the girls as they reached the prison's first floor. "In fact, I know she hasn't," said Joe, hustling the family into a car which awaited them.

On this last day before the trial, the district attorney insisted he and his staff had gathered the strongest evidence for conviction, and asserted he would seek the death penalty. Local sentiment had it that he would not get it.

For one thing, though the case had been labeled a "sex murder," there was nothing, short of intimation, that this was true, but this did not deter the press from referring to Ada as Dr. Dreher's "paramour." Newsmen hoped to see the seamy side of the case once the trial commenced. What, of course, they meant, was the sex motive, that colorful cesspool that sold newspapers.

Parkerson would not commit as to what strategy the defense might employ. "Wait and see," he said. "All I have to say is that we are going to get an acquittal, and when we get through with the district attorney and the sheriff's office, those fellows will be sorry they have had so many photographs appear in the newspapers."

At every stop of the Southern Pacific passenger trains from New Orleans to Franklin, news butchers were heard to hawk their wares raucously. "Read all about the murder," and they shouted the name of the newspapers they vended—no need for the names of the accused, even children knew those.

In Lawyer Pecot's office defense counsel sat down to analyze what they had to work with. "Let's look at what we know, or think we know," said Parkerson. "There seems little doubt that Mrs. LeBoeuf wrote the note that brought Dr. Dreher to the rendezvous out there on the lake, or that she was the one who set it up with her husband. What does seem at issue is whether LeBoeuf fired the first shot. We can almost be certain that Dreher was in fear for his life, else he wouldn't have brought Beadle out there with him,"

Pecot agreed, "And we can assume that it was Beadle who fired the shots which killed LeBoeuf. It was just as dark was setting in, and the Doc has no sight in that left eye, so surely he, from an unsteady seat in a small boat, was not the one. Beadle is the accomplished hunter and marksman. Whichever, it was self defense."

"All well and good," said Walker," but how do we explain the mutilation?"

"Look at it this way. It was panic," said Parkerson. "After LeBoeuf was killed, they knew that if they brought the body into town, the self-defense angle would be suspect in light of the enmity that existed between Doc and LeBoeuf, even between Beadle and LeBoeuf. If they left the body in the boat to be found, again they would be the suspects. No, they had to fix things so the body was not found and the way to do that was to eviscerate the body and weight it down."

"But which one did what?" Pecot asked.

"Good question," Walker said. "But that is the state's problem. They have to prove that one or the other did it, and it was Beadle for my money—he has the quick temper, he has the sharp eye, and he is the hunter who knows how to field dress a deer. It seems to me that the prosecution has its work cut out for them. We can be sure they have witnesses who can place our clients at the scene, but no one saw the killing, or they would have come forward by now. In the absence of that, all they have is circumstantial evidence, and I can't see a jury convicting on that!" They continued to work tirelessly into the night devising their strategy for opening day of the trial.

In the jail, their clients tossed and turned. They got little sleep on those thin cotton mattresses over the steel cots. The iron floors of their cells reverberated with every sound—the railroad cars being switched at the station, and in quieter moments even the crickets and buzz of mosquitoes outside the screens on the barred windows. In between came the croaking of the bullfrogs alongside the bayou.

8

Monday, July 25, 1927

Ada, the Doc, and Beadle woke Monday to the sounds of a summer rain, not a driving, hard rain, but one with a persistent, monotonous "plop" against the windows, indicated that it would be with them all day. Pewter clouds heightened the gloom of the trial's first day.

Deputy Arthur Martel, very big and important-looking, stood at the courthouse door counting how many of the courtroom seats remained, determined that the number set by the judge would not be exceeded. That maximum did not deter townsfolk and the curious who began well before 8 a. m. to come in droves, staking out front row seats in the clean, white-walled courtroom with its plain oak furnishings. Even the Negro population was intrigued by prospects of the trial, huddling in the far end of the gallery, resplendent in pink flop hats and blue shirts and similar finery.

At five minutes past 9 a. m., Chief Justice Charles O'Niell came into the chamber. The State Supreme Court's presiding judge was on vacation, away from the hurly-burly of New Orleans where the high court sat. He carried a gold-headed cane, yet walked still with a limp. Judge Simon and State Senator Provost rushed to greet him. It was almost like obsequious novice actors paying homage to the veteran.

There was a bustle on the floor and spectators stood in the balcony straining to see as the defendants entered the courtroom: Ada in her famous black satin dress and a white hat above her white powdered face, without too much rouge; James Beadle in a dark blue coat and black mohair trousers, wearing horn-rimmed glasses and chewing gum, and the Doc, in a gray suit and also chewing gum. Beadle sat between Ada and the Doc.

Shortly after the trial opened, Mrs. Dreher came in with her son, Ted, and nephew, Eugene Dreher. She sat by the side of her husband, silent, almost tragic. She was small and delicate, with a refined air, contrasting with the more buxom Ada. She was simply dressed in a dark blue georgette dress with silk sleeves offset by a beige collar and cuffs and a close-fitting beige hat over her smooth gray hair. Her shoes were high-heeled patent leather. She wore a strand of pearls, but her only other jewelry were her wedding and engagement rings. Mrs. Dreher sat quietly by her husband. Now and then she twisted the rings on her fingers, or played with her handbag, or pushed back a real or imagined stray hair.

Dr. Dreher appeared more at ease, perhaps, than some of the witnesses, even somewhat bored. He rose to greet his brother, D. M. Dreher of Clinton, a lean, lank, somewhat dour individual, when he entered and sat near him. It was almost a welcome break in the tedious proceedings of the opening trial.

Ada followed every word of the preliminaries attentively, though now and again her lips moved nervously, forming silent words. What words? What was she thinking at this point? Her face was immobile, expressionless.

Beadle chewed vigorously on his gum, paying rapt, schoolboy attention to the judge, occasionally grinning as though he felt he had already won his case.

Defense counsel first sought a continuance of the trial based largely on the absence of a missing witness, Robert Toerner, who reportedly would testify that he met Jim LeBoeuf the day of the murder, that Jim was armed and spoke of an appointment later with Dr. Dreher from whom he expected trouble. Toerner was reported to be in New Orleans and possibly enroute to Franklin.

Vuillemot, however, said he would attempt to impeach that testimony, if offered, as hearsay. In any event, despite a claim by the defense that it backed their contention of self-defense, the district attorney said all Toerner's testimony could show was that LeBoeuf was armed earlier that day.

Parkerson pushed for the court to throw out the jury venire on the grounds there were no women on the jury, and state law was unconstitutional in view of the requirement they had to sign a statement that they wished to participate in the jury process. By accepting that view, Judge Simon would, in effect, be transferring the trial to federal court. He overruled the motion, as well as numerous others entered by the defense, time-consuming motions which used up the judicial day.

The defense found that, for some reason, four names were duplicated in the venire. This meant, the attorneys contended, that because the panel was shy four of the 300. It was a disadvantage to the defendants. It was obvious, they said, that four of the panel represented eight men, and if the defense chose to challenge three of them, even one, obviously the defense would be charged with three (or one) challenges.

Judge Simon weighed through overruling the motion, and Parkerson objecting and filing a bill of exception. By the time the night session closed, only six venire men had been examined. Of these, one, William

Bartel, was selected for the jury, five were excused. Of these, four were dismissed for cause, one on a peremptory challenge.

Tuesday, July 26, 1927

The day would be a tiring one with repetitious questions directed to venire men, prospective jurors who would decide the fate of the three defendants. It would also be a long day: Judge Simon, anxious to complete the trial, decreed that the court would hold two sessions daily, one from 9 a. m. to 5 p. m., the second from 7 to 11 p. m.

Ada arrived in a new outfit, a black and white voile with a white organdy rolled collar ending on her right shoulder in a bow, the long ends of which extended almost to her waist, and organdy cuffs tied in chic little bows on her wrists. Her collar and cuffs were picoted on the edges with fine black thread. Together with her white felt hat and high-heeled, one-strap patent leather shoes, Ada looked younger and prettier than at any time since her arrest.

A woman reporter suggested, "Somebody ought to tell her to wear lipstick. Her pale lips against white makeup would prejudice any female onlooker." The reporter should have remembered there would be no females on the jury.

The same reporter observed, "Mrs. Dreher wore a new hat Tuesday, a soft little beige visca straw with a narrow line of navy blue grosgrain ribbon above the broad band of beige grosgrain ribbon around the crown. Her dress was the same that she had worn Monday, navy blue georgette over a figured silk slip, with a tiny bronze colored cluster of silk flowers pinned to her left shoulder. Her bag was of black leather, fastened with a cut crystal knob."

Behind the doctor and his wife, sat their son, Ted, and his two sisters, Dorothy and Polly. Dorothy was very slim and dark, sort of an Irish brunette with black hair and blue eyes. She wore a black dress with a brilliant orange scarf loosely tied across her shoulder. Her hair was closely bobbed with a rakish curl on either cheek in front of large pearls she wore in either ear. She wore a narrow strand of pearls, a thin gold bracelet on one wrist, a silver slave chain on the other. Pale fawn colored kid gauntlets completed her ensemble. Polly, a chubby little blonde, was dressed in white, a blue silk hat over her golden hair. About her shoulders she wore a brightly colored scarf.

About 10 a. m. Joe LeBoeuf, eldest of Ada's three sons, came into court and she gave him a chair next to hers. Wrote a reporter: "He is a handsome young fellow, looking more like a sophomore enjoying a summer between the arduous seasons of football and frat rushing than like a boy whose father has been murdered, and his mother, accused of illicit love for another man, stands in the shadow of the gallows."

The lone juror, Bartel, chosen Monday night, sat fidgeting in the otherwise empty jury box, swinging from side to side in his swivel chair, looking self conscious.

As the prosecution questioned prospective jurors, Parkerson objected to the judge that when the prosecution asked prospective jurors in the event the state proved its case, "would you bring in a verdict that would sentence the accused to the gallows.

"The word should be 'could' not 'would,'" Parkerson said, "because if the juror promised he 'would' bring in a verdict that must be followed by capital punishment, that would prevent his qualifying a verdict so as to prevent a capital sentence." Judge Simon agreed and so instructed the prosecution.

Nonetheless, the district attorney persisted in using "would" in his questioning, and each time Parkerson jumped to his feet to object. Over and over, Simon repeated his ruling. Each time, Vuillemot, whether it was because he "could" not or "would" not remember, smiled and corrected himself. At one point, the district attorney said humorously, "I forgot what the word was."

By noon, the defense entered seven of its 36 allowed peremptory challenges, the state six of its 18 before the lunch recess. The jury selection process, dull as it was, did not thin the ranks of the audience. Attorneys posed the same or identical questions to each venire man, and received almost identical responses, "Are you opposed to capital punishment?—No.—Would you be willing to inflict it in this case?—Yes.—Would the fact that one of the defendants is a woman make any difference as to a vote to hang?—No.

Court Clerk Wilbur Kramer told newsmen, "Men from country districts make convincing jurors and are ready to hang." Even if it meant that if convicted, Ada Bonner LeBoeuf would become the first woman to be legally executed in the state of Louisiana.

The afternoon session dragged on and on. The audience grew restive, largely because they could not understand the proceedings, and in part due to the intense heat. They broke out their thermos containers of ice water and tea, fanning vigorously with cardboard hand fans generously furnished by local merchants and the funeral parlor, all bearing their advertising and colorful religious scenes, or dried palmetto fans brought from home.

It was inevitable that the trial would run into language barriers. St. Mary Parish was located in Cajun country, many of its citizens being descendants of those early settlers, many still speaking a jargon reminiscent of the language of their forefathers, a hint of music and loud. Whenever the speaker had no ready word in French, he would substitute the English, then proceed in French.

The defense had accepted Louis Fouquier as a juror, but the prosecution complained that he did not understand enough English to be sure of what the fuss was all about. Sure, he knew the lady was being tried for the murder of her husband. "Then, do you understand what I mean when I say that a man is presumed innocent until proved guilty?" asked Judge Simon.

"Yes, sir."

L. O. Pecot said to Judge Simon that Fouquier understood English as well as the judge himself. Simon turned to Fouquier and asked, "Do you understand what is meant by 'a reasonable doubt', Mr. Fouquier?" After some hesitation, Fouquier shook his head side to side, and defense attorney agreed that a man who didn't know what "reasonable doubt" was couldn't sit on the jury.

Next is was the turn of the district attorney when L. J. Walker was called. Walker had been the barber who shaved both Dr. Dreher and Jim Beadle. Vuillemot worried that he might have become attached to them, and although Walker vehemently denied it, he was not accepted. As a local barber, Walker had discussed the case often enough with his customers, said the prosecution.

Tension piggy-backed tedium as proceedings grew grim. Dissatisfied with progress in jury selection, Judge Simon announced that he would hold the court in session until four in the morning if it was necessary to fill the jury box.

Attorneys for both sides desperately tried to find ways to discharge jurors not to their liking for cause rather than expending their dwindling quota by peremptory challenges. Prospective jurors were not helping matters. Three of them, not understanding legal technicalities, laid themselves open to dismissal for cause. Parkerson, for the defense, doggedly filed bills of exception at every opportunity, building his case for later appeal. As if to vent his frustration, Judge Simon joined the gum chewers.

The venire exhausted, Sheriff Pecot and his deputies were sent to round up a special tales jury of 90 drawn from the box in open court before the start of the night session. Twenty-seven of those were excused, or had moved or left the parish. Nineteen failed to answer in court when their names were called, leaving 44 available to the attorneys for questioning. But the defense objected to proceeding.

"Suppose three names were called, the names of three men acceptable to the defense and none of them answered," suggested defense attorney L. O. Pecot. "The injury to our case would be obvious."

If that was lost to the lay reasoning, it also escaped the legal mind of Judge Simon. He overruled the objection and ordered the case to go forward. Parkerson filed another exception and three tales jurors were called. B. A. Coyeault was excused for cause by the state when he became the first prospective juror to say he was opposed to capital punishment. Two others failed to make it to the jury box.

A newsman observed that outside the railing demarking the courtroom, many of the area's prettiest, in their dating finery, sat with their escorts, making it, to them, a social event. To them, the Opera House and its silent movies, well might have been dark. The boys were happy that the state was furnishing entertainment that cost them nothing.

A reporter for the *Times-Picayune* observed:

> The proper way to make a date these days, as accepted by the flaming youth of Franklin, is no longer 'Wanna take a ride?' or any other of the outworn phrases in vogue of yore. It is 'Let's go piroguing'. . . . though the lawyers voices grew husky, though the stenographers and newspaper reporters twisted their fingers to ward off writer's cramp, though even Judge Simon mopped his brow and sighed, the onlookers sat in their places, tireless as wallflowers waiting to be asked to dance.

Whether it was their own tiredness, or whether it was a growing irritability on the part of Judge Simon, as the night session dragged on, two more jurors were chosen; Theodore Dumesnil, a farmer from Asion, and Paul Fangue, a Rhoda farmer, bringing the number of jurors to three. By this time the regular venire was exhausted and seeing the special tales jury panning out so poorly, Judge Simon signed an order to the jury commissioners to supplement the tales jurors in their box so that it would contain a full complement of one hundred names when court convened the next morning.

Wednesday, July 27, 1927

Wednesday portended even more monotony. Ada appeared in a cool and refreshing white handkerchief linen dress, a Peter Pan collar and cuffs with black piping, tied at the waist with a narrow sash of black ribbon. A woman reporter observed that thus far Ada had worn no color to court. But she must have read accounts of her Tuesday court appearance—today her lips had a light pink tinge and so also did her cheeks—the rouge had been ever so lightly applied, but it was there.

By her side sat Ernest LeBoeuf, a son, clad in a crisp linen suit, and just behind them was Ben Blakeman, her nephew, and Emory Bonner, her brother. While she talked cheerfully with all three, she firmly clasped Ernest's hand, never loosing it for but maybe a minute at the time, interlacing their fingers, resting their hands on the arm of her chair. Ernest was 16, tanned and handsome, almost a mirror image of his mother, but masculine—he was captain of the Morgan City High School football team. He appeared devoted to his mother.

Doc and Beadle had on the same suits they wore the day before, but Beadle wore a new tie.

Mrs. Dreher, sitting by her husband, wore the same dress she had on the day before, but she had exchanged the pearls for a necklace of the palest lavender crystals. Polly highlighted her golden hair with a yellow hat, and a yellow georgette batik scarf. Her older sister, Dorothy, seemed distant in her midnight blue georgette, a cluster of bright orange flowers at her shoulder. Both sisters had won the reputation for being aloof with the press, in exhibiting a rude politeness in curt responses to newsmen's questions.

Court did not open until 10:40 a. m., though it had been announced for 10 a. m. Word circulated that Judge Simon was not feeling well, but though he seemed sluggish in his walk and his face was a little drawn, he opened court without reference to his health.

A drizzly summer rain had begun at about 8 a. m. and continued as court convened. Onlookers who had awakened before dawn to travel the backroads to be here were not prepared to give up their seats and return home at this juncture, despite the fact that most did not understand the pre-trial proceedings.

Mrs. Dreher sat rigidly, her hands tightly folded in her lap. Dorothy leaned forward, resting one arm on the back of the doctor's chair, and the other gently stroking his arm. Once he reached back and clasped her hand. Polly was closely following juror questioning. She had big black circles under eyes, and from time to time looked resentfully around the courtroom, as if to say "What are you doing to my father and why?"

Crumpled in a chair behind Ada was Mrs. Husband, Jim LeBoeuf's mother, dressed in deep mourning, a black veil over her bowed head. She wept as attorneys harangued. Finally, after an hour and a half of listening to examination of venire men, the aged woman collapsed, sobbing audibly, and had to be helped from the courtroom. Judge Simon recessed proceedings and Sheriff Pecot had a deputy drive her home.

When court resumed late in the afternoon, two more jurors were selected: N. A. Barilleaux of Centerville, a mechanic, and Joseph L. DeLaune, Patterson sawmill employee. And still the questioning continued.

"Half of them [the venire men] don't even know what the word 'indictment' means," Judge Simon complained. He was ill, but devoted to his duty. He let proceedings go to 4 p. m., but finally was unable to continue. He canceled the night session. The Opera House had its patrons back, at least for the night.

Thursday, July 28, 1927

Mrs. C. E. Bonner, Ada's mother, was among early arrivals Thursday morning, her aged face already showing the trail of tears down her lined cheeks. She was given a seat just behind Ada and between two of her sons, one of whom, Emory, gently stroked her withered arm. Her ill-fitting dress was homemade.

Softly, almost timidly, she leaned forward, leaning her head on her daughter's shoulder, her lips moving tremulously, almost convulsively, and now and again she sobbed, her tears streaking down the sleeve of Ada's crisp voile dress. Mrs. Bonner listened as again and again the attorneys asked venire men "And could you render a verdict that would send a woman to the gallows?," grueling questions bespeaking her daughter's possible fate, such as "Could you try a woman just as you would a man? . . . You are sure that pity or sympathy for her would not affect you?"

The heat, her age, her emotions, the interminable questions, all added to what had to be breakdown. She did not possess Ada's iron control. At length, she could no longer contain her grief. Emory, his arms around her waist, led her weeping uncontrollably from the courtroom, clearing the way through the curious who congested the aisle.

For the first time, Beadle was surrounded by his family in court, his wife and five of their seven children—Calvin, 21; Irene, 18; Holden, 16; Wilson, 11; Pleasant, 9. They left at home Lester, 23, and Byron, 20. Mrs. Alice Beadle, brunette, slender and petite, looked hardly old enough to have a son of voting age. She came to court over her physician's protest. For years she had had a weak heart, and her doctor was fearful the trial would tax her strength. Irene, pretty in pink dress and hat, sat to one side of her mother, her brother, Calvin sunburned from following his father in hunting and trapping, on the other. The two youngest boys sat in chairs to their rear, twisting and turning out of boredom with the proceedings they didn't understand. Pleasant found some excitement in fingering a loose tooth.

Recovered from her previous visit, Mrs. Husband was back again, like a figurine in a Black Forest clock emerging on the hour, reluctant to relinquish her spot in the limelight and the opportunity to disparage her daughter-in-law. She told newsmen outside the courthouse,

> Ada was a poor housekeeper and a worse cook. My poor boy hardly ate at home at all for the past year. He never said anything, but they tell me he used to eat at restaurants all the time. And when I went to see them, I used to carry my lunch in a paper bag because I never could tell when she was going to have a hot meal and when she wasn't. She used to give the children nothing but grits and butter for supper, and Jim never did eat butter, not even when he was a little fellow. But I wanted him to stay with her for the children's sake. The little girl, Liberty, is just 8 years old and she's just like a baby.

As she trudged away, a bystander snickered and said, "Ada's cooking might not win any prizes at the church fair, but if her kids look like that only on grits and butter, I'm gonna change my youngsters' eating habits."

Vuillemot, too, spoke with newsmen. He announced that he had no intention of dwelling on sexual details in the case, but was more interested in crimes rather than motives.

Court opened with holdover exceptions from Parkerson, such as destruction of the names of tales jurors who had failed to answer to their names when called Wednesday night. The jury commission reported it had completed the job of adding names to the tales jury box and the full complement of one hundred had been reached. The rest of the morning went routinely. Emilion Savoie of Franklin became a member of the jury, and then Hipolite Bodin, also of Franklin.

Back in court, at 1:43 p.m., the attorneys continued their task of selecting a jury. They heard the same replies . . . tales jurors were opposed to capital punishment, they had too strong an opinion as to guilt or innocence, *ad infinitum.*

Shortly into the afternoon session, Judge Simon invited the opposing attorneys into his chambers. There was a problem, he suggested, with one of the jurors, Fangue. Investigation showed he had lied during his questioning: prior to his voire dire, Fangue had made remarks in front of several witnesses at a country store that he and members of his family had been treated by Dr. Dreher again and again, and had never received a bill for his services. Fangue told his friends, "I'll hang them but not Dr. Dreher." In his voir dire, however, Fangue had said he had no scruples against capital punishment as applied to any of the defendants. Both prosecution and defense attorneys concurred with Simon—Fangue had to be removed, though Vuillemot said he would not prosecute Fangue for perjury.

Two more jurors were accepted, O. J. Simoneaux, a Charenton farmer and father of thirteen children, and Richard Wilkes, a Foster storekeeper. Vuillemot got a smothered laugh from spectators when, questioning Simoneaux, he asked as to his accomplishment as a parent: "Is that all?"

Wilkes confessed he might be worried about his business while on jury duty, but Judge Simon said "Jury service is one of the most sacred duties."

The attorneys were about to run out of tales jurors; of the latest 100, 56 answered their names. By 4 p. m., 18 had been examined and 3 accepted. But the defense had used 25 of its peremptories, 11 remaining, and the state only had 3, having used 15.

Following a short recess, the next juror, Ferdinand Estele, from Garden City, was being questioned. His understanding of English was limited, and attorneys for both sides were laboriously explaining matters, a persistent problem throughout the jury selection process. On direct examination Estele said he spoke mostly French. L. O. Pecot, for the defense, drew from Estele that he did not know the meaning of the word "indictment." Vuillemot immediately objected to further questioning and moved to dismiss Estele for cause.

Judge Simon, by this time exasperated by the slow process and the inability of prospective jurors to serve because of problems with the language, ruled that it was not necessary for a juror to know the meaning of "indictment."

"The district attorney objected too soon. I was about to explain the meaning of the word," said Pecot, holding aloft a piece of paper. "An indictment is a piece of paper with writing on it. It would be read to you in court and it will charge so and so."

Estele smiled. Judge Simon added him to the jury.

Prospective juror Paul Bodin of Franklin was asked by the defense if he would understand what was meant if the statement were made "he came to his death . . . in a willful and felonious manner. Do you understand that?"

"Yes."

"What do you understand is meant by 'willful'?"

"It means he is dead, huh?"

There were titters in the courtroom.

"You don't understand what 'felonious' means?"

"No, sir."

"If you don't understand that, how could you understand the law as the judge would charge you? If he used the same words I have used, you would not understand that, would you?"

Pecot moved to challenge Bodin for cause, but Judge Simon asked Bodin, "Do you speak English or do you just understand it?"

"I speak it, yes sir. Plain English, but I don't understand some big words."

Simon continued: "If you were seated as a juror, do you think you could understand the testimony?"

"Yes, sir, no trouble at all."

Judge Simon threw out the challenge.

In the continued voir dire proceedings, most of the peremptory challenges were exhausted until the jury was complete. L. S. Alleman of Garden City and John Bonin were selected within half an hour after examination of tales jurors resumed. Fangue was purged from the jury on motion of Judge Simon and with the consent of both prosecutor and defense counsel.

With completion of the jury, the way was now clear for the trial to begin. Observers could not tell whether it was relief showing on the faces of the defendants or not.

9

Friday, July 29, 1927

Before dawn, pushing, shoving, treading on one another's toes, jabbing each other in the ribs, they sought to win one of the coveted expanded 510 seats in the courtroom. Last night the jury was completed. Today would mark the main event as the trial itself was scheduled to begin.

Chief Justice Charles O'Niell, who had been sitting in as a visitor, estimated this to be the largest crowd ever to witness a trial in Louisiana. Every seat was taken by 8 a. m. After that, it was a free-for-all scuffle as the crowd continued to grow, wedging bodies between the seats and the walls, spilling into the aisles, overflowing into the corridor, down the front steps onto the courthouse lawn. They infringed on the space assigned the press and had to be dislodged physically by sheriff's deputies. The estimate was close to a thousand crammed in where only 300 were meant to be. The state and defense attorneys had to shoulder their way through the throng.

Outwardly as untroubled as in recent days, the three defendants made their way into the court—Ada in a new dress of lavender and white figured percale with a black ribbon bow which pinned at the neck. Her son, Ernest, and nieces, Vivian Blakeman and Dot Boudreaux, accompanied her.

Mrs. Dreher was at her husband's side, dressed in blue figured crepe de chine, together with daughters Polly and Dorothy and son Ted.

Shortly after 10 a.m., Sheriff Pecot called court to order and spectators settled back expectant that testimony would begin. But one of the jurors, A. J. Boudreaux, was excused and the process of picking his replacement began. The spectators did not budge from their places. They had risen early and come far and would not leave willingly. Judge Simon simply said Boudreaux was excused. No reason. Report circulated, however, that while still a tales juror, he had made statements that he wanted the chance to hang a man of Dr. Dreher's religious and fraternal affiliations.

Parkerson was forced to ask the court "for a chair to sit down in," the crush of onlookers was so great. Juror selection continued until Sidney Pitre, of Ashton, was seated. By noon the court recessed, to reconvene later in the afternoon. When it did, it was almost 3:50 p. m.

Dr. Horton, parish corner, led the early parade of witnesses, telling in cold medical terms the macabre story eagerly awaited by the spectators. He was followed by Charles Burgers, Jr., who described the stumpy thumbs and peculiar small finger nails by which he had identified James LeBoeuf's body. Next came Morgan City Police Chief Blakeman, brother-in-law of the deceased, who said he had known LeBoeuf for 23 years, and was able to identify him, even without the stubby thumbs. Further identification was that of LeBoeuf's shoes.

The identification process apparently complete, the state called Lufr Trahan, 15, a tanned youngster, obviously curious as to the proceedings, looking around the court, wide-eyed, between questions, who testified he had seen Dr. Dreher and Beadle in Dr. Dreher's car, with a boat lashed to the side just at dusk on July 1.

"Whose boat did you see?"

"Jim Beadle's."

"Who was driving the car?"

"Dr. Dreher."

"You saw them at dusk with the boat?"

"Yes."

"You've never had any trouble with Dr. Dreher, have you?"

"No, sir."

"You haven't got a grudge or anything against him, have you?"

"No, sir."

"In which direction was he driving?"

"North."

"Was that section of town dry or wet [from the recent flood]?"

"Dry."

"Was the section around the schoolhouse dry or wet?"

"It was wet behind."

"Did you see them afterward?"

"No."

Lufr's younger brother, Morris, 13, repeated the story of the boat on the car, as did Odette and Jeanne Theriot. Mrs. Philip Vicnair was questioned.

"Were you at home on July 1?"

"Yes, sir."

"Were you on the front porch?"

"Yes, sir."

"Was the sun up? How long did you stay there, an hour, half an hour?"

"Half an hour."

"Did you see Beadle in Dr. Dreher's car?"

"Yes, sir."

"When was the last time you saw them together?"

"Quite a while."

"Did you ever see anyone come to the corner of the schoolhouse with a pirogue on the side of the car?"

"Yes."

"Did you see them put the pirogue in the water?"

"Yes, sir."

"Did you recognize those with it?"

"I recognized Dr. Dreher."

"Did you ever see that green pirogue before?"

"Yes, sir, during the high water."

"When did you see Dr. Dreher and Jim Beadle near the schoolhouse?"

"On Friday, July 1."

"About what time?"

"About 6:30 p.m."

Thus, the district attorney placed the Doc and Beadle together, with the green pirogue about early dusk near the schoolhouse.

Alec Comeaux, who lived near the schoolhouse, testified he had heard two shots the night of July 1 at about 8 p. m.

"And are you positive you heard two shots?" Vuillemot asked.

"Yes."

"You have been a hunter, Mr. Comeaux?"

"All my life."

"Do you hunt now?"

"No."

"Too old?"

"No. No more game."

"Can you tell the difference between a pistol shot, a rifle shot, and a shotgun shot?"

"Yes."

"Were the two shots you heard made by a pistol, a shotgun, or a rifle?"

"By a shotgun."

"How far apart did you hear the two shots?"

"About half a second."

Whether it was the heat or that the day had been tedious, but for the first time Ada proved she had nerves and that there was a breaking point. Suddenly she pitched forward in her chair, almost collapsing on the floor. Sheriff Pecot rushed forward. "Give her air," he shouted, reaching for a glass of water which he held to her lips. Ernest frantically used a cardboard fan to shovel breezes to her pale, wan face. She recovered in about 15 minutes before court mercifully adjourned until Saturday morning.

Saturday, July 30, 1927

During Friday night a heavy rain battered the area, a factor which thinned the crowd Saturday morning. Still all available seats were occupied and scores of onlookers stood. Ada looked decidedly fresher than she did after the 15 hours of heat and testimony caused her collapse the previous night. She sat quietly, unaware that her son, Ernest, and nephew Ben Blakeman, had entered the courtroom until a chair was pulled along side her. She smiled, slipped her hand into his, and swallowed hard. Ernest placed a protective arm around her shoulder, his cheek close to hers.

The state called its first witness, the elusive Robert Toerner whose absence had prompted the defense earlier to seek a continuance, saying he could testify that he had seen James LeBoeuf with a black automatic pistol the evening of July 1.

Toerner said that while the country was being scoured for him, he was unaware of the search, that he was in Port Arthur, Texas, looking for a job when he read in the newspaper that he was wanted as a witness in a murder case, and he went immediately to the Port Arthur police station.

The witness proved a fizzle after opposing counsel wrangled while the jury was sent from the room. Toerner declared he knew nothing of the case and had not seen LeBoeuf with a pistol as claimed by the defense. The heated exchange of the attorneys was as bewildering to the witness as it was the rest of the courtroom. He was finally excused, shuffling from the witness stand with a look which seemed to say, "Why was I ever brought here?"

In that Ada had doubted the body to be that of her husband, the state offered a motion to exhume the body. All three defendants were visibly shaken by the announcement.

Vuillemot said E. C. Kiplinger, the undertaker, could not appear in court. But the story circulated that perhaps the body might not be exhumed after it was known that Morgan City dentist A. K. White was summoned to bring the impression from which LeBoeuf's dentures were made. Dr. White sent word, however, that he could not identify the impression. Before the end of the morning session, the motion to exhume the body was withdrawn.

During the noon recess, Pecot confirmed to reporters that he had received a letter from a Baton Rouge palmist who insisted that Beadle was innocent. She said to get an answer, she had consulted her cards, reshuffling them seven times. Each time, the answer was the same.

"You have in your town undergoing trial an innocent man," she wrote to the sheriff.

> I, a palmist, shuffled the cards to find the true murderers in the LeBoeuf case. Seven times straight the cards showed Jim Beadle innocent. It

> showed Dr. Dreher fired the shot [*sic*] and used the knife. Mrs. LeBoeuf did not leave the scene of the murder as stated. She assisted Dr. Dreher until the last, kissed him good-bye, and then satisfied each other that their troubles were over.

Unfortunately for Beadle, the court did not take such "testimony" into consideration.

The afternoon session opened with Ada sitting quietly, a blue handkerchief pressed to her lips. Beadle chewed his gum stolidly. Dreher leaned his head on his hands, but listened intently as Sheriff Pecot was questioned about the confession said to have been made by Ada the day of her arrest. Again the jury had been sent from the room as Pecot testified. The defense protested vigorously introduction of testimony as to the confession the state claimed was made to Sheriff Pecot.

Ada seemed to show a flicker of nervousness. She sat stonily rigid while the sheriff told of searching her home for a rifle as she assisted him. There was an occasional twitch in her fingers as she held her handkerchief close to her face. She listened as Pecot recited her reaction to her husband's absence—that he frequently was gone from home days at a time—that she did not believe the body found in Lake Palourde was that of her husband. He told how she had broken down and admitted she had been lying, how she had confessed knowledge of the crime, her presence at the scene, but her denial that she knew the men in the other boat who had fired at her husband.

Police Chief Blakeman, Ada's brother-in-law, said he had not promised Ada leniency when he urged her to turn state's evidence. Blakeman corroborated Pecot's account of Ada's statement following initial questioning. Again, Ada's first day confession was examined endlessly and repetitiously before the day drew to a close and promised a Sunday respite.

10

Sunday, July 31, 1927

Peeling church bells early Sunday broke what slumber there was for Ada, the Doc, and Beadle. The crowds that almost suffocated them in previous days now took themselves to church, leaving the jail house quiet except for the peaceful chirping of birds outside.

From his cell window, Doc saw the slow moving brown waters of the Teche. He could estimate the current by the movement of the water hyacinths and their purple blooms lazily carried on its surface.

In the ground fog which still lingered near the bank, stilt-legged herons extended their long necks to fish minnows from the bayou, their white feathers blending with the snowy plumes of egrets gracefully gliding from the tops of spindly cypresses already losing their needles in late summer. The birds were probably migrants from the McIlhenny bird sanctuary on Avery Island, just southwest of Franklin.

Despite the heat outside, a chill pervaded the jail, primarily because of the thick masonry walls insulating the interior. The morning sun was only now invading the cellblocks through the narrow exterior windows, casting ominous shadows of the bars on surfaces within. It was the only connection with the outside world.

Dreher had always been an early riser, anyway, and he took advantage of the morning to exercise in the jail corridor, one of the privileges Sheriff Pecot had accorded to him. Still, within their cells, each one paced the small space allotted, but anticipating on this day of rest, the first they had since the trial began, that after Sunday dinner, they would be allowed visitors.

Absent were the gymnast onlookers who literally climbed the columns supporting the domed ceiling in the circular little courtroom built to handle 300 but which was accommodating more than three times that number, a room which had absorbed the odors of chewing gum, over ripe bananas, and bologna sandwiches, of women's perfumes, and field-hand sweat.

Pecot allowed Ada to keep a rocking chair in her cell. She used it that Sunday, the noise against the iron floor echoing through the jail, as she awaited the first of her visitors, members of her family, Ada's mother,

Opposite page, upper left: Dr. Thomas Dreher, Ada LeBoeuf, and James Beadle shortly after their arrests. Above, Sheriff Charles Pecot.

Editor's note: The poor quality of the images results from copying old newspaper pictures. No glossy prints or negatives of the principals in the case could be located.

Above: The site of the murder.

Below: Sheriff Pecot escorts Ada LeBoeuf to court.

Above: A courtroom scene with Ada LeBoeuf on the stand.
Left: Ada LeBoeuf shortly before execution.
Right: Dr. Dreher, shortly before execution, being escorted by Sheriff Charles Pecot.
Below: The St. Mary Parish Couthouse, where the LeBoeuf - Dreher case was tried.

dragging the weight of her 75 years up the steps to Ada's third floor cell. She was among the first to arrive.

As she left the jail she sobbed aloud. "My poor child has suffered so, so much and so long," she said as she stumbled from Ada's cell. She told reporters:

> She was so pitifully unhappy with Jim LeBoeuf. He wasn't good to her. Ada's a good girl, a good girl. They say such horrible things about her, but I can't believe them. Ada is not bad.
>
> I am an old woman, and people have been telling me a long time that I ought to stop work, but I can't. I keep that coffee shop in Morgan City so I won't be a drag on my children. I couldn't add to Ada's burden because you know Ada isn't strong. She has a tumor. The doctor told her that three years ago. She should have had an operation long before this. Ada's a sick woman now and this trial is more than she can stand. I don't see how she can bear up.
>
> I tell you, Ada is sick. If she doesn't have an operation soon—oh, if something isn't done for my girl and this dreadful affair goes on like this, she can't stand it. She can't. If the jury does declare her guilty, she will die before they can . . . before they can do anything to her. I know.

Her feeble old voice broke and she began to weep openly and with no restraint.

Several blocks away, lounging newsmen, from the gallery of the Commercial Hotel, stopped passing town folk to ask their opinions as to the progress of the trial and their expectations of the outcome. In most cases the people were stern when they spoke of the trial. They had crowded into the courtroom and gawked at the defendants and they were almost unanimous that the jury would not return a verdict to hang Ada. Many predicted a mistrial. "They won't hang Ada," one said. "She's a woman and more than that, she's the kind of woman they won't hang. She isn't beautiful. Few women who have done their own housework for twenty years are, but she has that something, you know. She won't hang and she knows it. That's why she's so quiet."

While there was a certain amount of sympathy for Beadle, even for Dr. Dreher, there was none for Ada. Men and women alike deplored her alleged straying from her marital vows. The Roaring Twenties may have relaxed moral standards elsewhere, but those lowered levels of conduct had not reached the backwaters of Louisiana. Everywhere Ada looked she saw curiosity, condemnation, and contempt.

There were exceptions, her mother and Ernest. Anyone who looked at Ernest in that stifling courtroom knew he would always stand by his mother. His devotion was obvious as he held her hand, put his arm around her shoulder in such a protective way. He was loyal to Ada, no matter how hot the courtroom, how long and tedious the testimony. Ernest was there. Ada needed him, and he knew it.

To break the monotony—and take advantage of the presence of newsmen not occupied with the trial on this "day of rest,"—Defense Counsel Parkerson held a news conference in the afternoon. He again asked the public to withhold its verdict, not to condemn blindly before all the evidence was in.

11

Monday, August 1, 1927

The "woman across the tracks"—Ada never named her—started it all.

Ada sat on the edge of her tumbled cot, clad in her bungalow apron, the first rays of sunlight edging past the bars of her cell. Three reporters sat with their stenographic pads and pencils at the ready.

It was Monday morning of perhaps the most fateful day of the trial, a day when the decision was expected on whether her confession would be admitted into evidence, and she had agreed to talk to three New Orleans reporters: Martha Dalrymple of the *Item*; Meigs O. Frost of the *States*; and Gwen Bristow of the *Times-Picayune*. She told them: "It was that anonymous 'woman across the tracks.'" Ada said she knew her but declined to name the person who wrote Mrs. Dreher and accused Ada and Dr. Dreher of having illicit relations.

Mrs. Dreher took the letters (there were several) to Jim LeBoeuf at his office at the power plant. That precipitated two years of unbearable torture by an insanely jealous husband. "Maybe they won't let me talk, but I want to talk. I want to tell the truth—how I had wanted Jim and the doctor to meet on the lake and get things settled in a friendly way. I had to do something to end the hell I had lived for those two years but Jim's jealousy drove him mad. He carried a pistol that night. He cursed the doctor and told him he had better keep away from me. Then he fired. Somebody fired back. I am sure it was not the doctor. He and Jim Beadle were in the other boat."

She paused, fingering the newspapers in her lap, newspapers with stories she had been reading before her interview and the trek to the courthouse. "These papers tell what other people have said about me. But I know what really happened. People have talked so much—if that woman across the track had not been one of these people who can't help bothering with other people's affairs, none of this would have been, not those terrible two years and this climax.

"My God, how I endured those two years! It was hell. Dr. Dreher had always been a good friend of my family. He brought my babies, and he always came to see us when there was sickness in the house. But Jim never dreamed of anything else—nobody else would have had anything to talk about if that woman across the track had minded her own business and not imagined things that weren't there. Jim was good to us. He adored the children and gave them everything they ever wanted. He was like that, devoted and quiet, a good husband to me and a good father to them until all of this started.

"I had been sick. You know I have a tumor and they say I need an operation. I suppose I'll have one if I ever get through with this. Dr. Dreher had been treating me. He came to the house and sometimes he would stay half an hour, sometimes an hour, just passing the time of day. You know, things that were happening among my friends and talking to the children. One day he came in looking grave.

"'You'd better hurry and get well, Ada,' he said. 'People are saying things about you and me. They say I come here too often.'

"Well, that worried me naturally, and I spoke to Jim about it, and it annoyed him, but there was no sign that he believed it. He told me I was sick and nervous, and not to bother about town gossip. Then, Mrs. Dreher began getting anonymous letters. I know who wrote them, but I'm not going to say because there are enough people mixed up in this ghastly affair already.

"Mrs. Dreher took the letters down to the plant where Jim worked and showed them to him, and Jim went wild. Since that day, God only knows the agony I have lived in. Jim forbade Dr. Dreher the house and forbade me to speak to him when he passed me on the street. The husband of the woman who had written Mrs. Dreher came to Jim to apologize for the mischief that his wife had done, for by that time the whole town was talking, and I couldn't cross the street without being grinned at.

"How those things go on in a small town. But apologies were no good. Those letters had done all the evil they were intended to do, and they were going to do more."

Ada stopped and passed her hand across her eyes as though to block out those memories. Her face looked haggard. She had not yet applied the makeup she generally wore in the courtroom. Then, she resumed her story.

"I had never known my husband could be like that. One day I went to Mrs. Dreher. Perhaps I shouldn't have gone, but I had to speak to her. The moment I mentioned her showing those letters to my husband, she stopped me. 'Mrs. LeBoeuf, can you forgive me for showing those letters to your husband?' I told her I would, of course. The mischief had been started and was already going too fast for her or for me to stop it. But there was no sense in saying so. I was tired. 'Forgive me,' she said again, and again I said I would.

"But the whole thing had gone beyond apologies. My husband's mind was poisoned, he saw meanings in the simplest doings of everyday life. At last, I came to the end of my endurance. I had to have it over.

"So I wrote to Dr. Dreher and asked him to meet my husband and me on Lake Palourde where we could tell my husband the truth of it all and have it done with."

Gwen Bristow interrupted. "Did you say in that letter, as you have been reported to say, 'you had better get him before he gets you?'"

"No," Ada replied. "I did not. I wanted them to talk together, quietly, where there would be no fear of interruption. I wanted my husband to hear the doctor's side and vice versa. I was desperate, but so was my husband. He carried a pistol. We met the doctor and James Beadle in the pirogue on the lake."

"Did you recognize them both, Mrs. LeBoeuf?" Frost asked.

"Oh yes," Ada answered.

"Had Beadle ever quarreled with your husband?" asked Dalrymple.

"I don't think so," Ada replied. She sat twisting the black bow pinned at her neck. Then, she continued her recollections, speaking slowly and carefully. "My husband had paddled up close to the doctor's pirogue and they began to talk. But in three minutes Jim LeBoeuf had lost his temper, and that jealousy and hatred buried within him for those two awful years broke out in one intense flash. Suddenly my husband snatched out his pistol and fired."

The interview ended abruptly when the jailer warned she had best get dressed because time was nearing for the defendants to be taken to the courtroom. She appeared to the reporters to be harried as they left her, preparing to slip from the bungalow apron into what she obviously had planned ahead of time to wear that day.

The day began with what spectators recognized as the near end of the trial as word spread that the hitherto inscrutable Jim Beadle had finally given Sheriff Pecot a confession. Pecot told the court that Beadle no longer wished to be represented by Parkerson and the defense team, but wanted his own counsel. He had no money, he told the court. Until that time, his defense costs had been borne by Dr. Dreher.

"The accused has been very ably represented," Judge Simon observed, but he appointed Rene H. Himel as new attorney to defend Beadle. C. A. Blanchard later volunteered to assist Himel. Beadle's decision shocked the defense and their clients. The trapper had given them no prior warning.

Through all of this action, the Doc followed proceedings as if Beadle had struck him physically. He continued to chew his gum calmly and deliberately, but his eyes betrayed a sudden fear even though his face did not show any emotion.

Ada, on the other hand, had a ghastly countenance, her face was contorted, drawn and white, almost as if she were in pain.

In essence, Beadle's confession related his version of what had happened, and his story was that Dr. Dreher had been the one to fire the fatal shots. The confession was admitted to the jury without protest from Beadle's new attorneys.

The prosecution already had two confessions from Ada: one she had made in Walter Gilmore's office in Morgan City and one she had dictated after being lodged in the St. Mary Parish jail, but which she had not signed because District Attorney Vuillemot had said it was not necessary. Both were before she was represented by counsel.

In the absence of the jury, the defense vigorously protested admission of either one, then about-faced to agree to them being admitted to the jury in an effort to show duress on the part of the state in obtaining them.

Vuillemot could not have caused more consternation for the defense team had he thrown a bomb under their chairs when he announced yet a third "confession" by Ada—that which she had so freely given to the three newspaper reporters that morning in her cell.

Thinking quickly, Parkerson summoned Frost and Dalrymple as witnesses for the defense. That meant that if he did not call them to testify, their account of the "press confession" could not be offered into evidence. The attorney was not concerned with Ada's assertion that Beadle had fired the fatal volley because he no longer represented Beadle. But what was disturbing to the defense was Ada's statement that she made the assignation on the lake. That would be difficult to explain to jurors.

Frost was reported to be ill, confined to his room at the Commercial Hotel with what appeared to be the early harbinger of an attack of appendicitis.

But Parkerson, in his zeal to exclude the "press confession," had reacted too quickly. He did not include the third reporter present at Ada's invitational press conference, Gwen Bristow. And Vuillemot pounced on this fact, summoning her as his witness.

In the afternoon session, the defense, with the jury excluded from the courtroom, tried valiantly to prohibit introduction of any of the confessions (except Beadle's) as all day jurors were marched in and out of the jury box while attorneys engaged in their legal pyrotechnics. Early in the night session, Dr. Dreher's confession was admitted into evidence.

Sheriff Pecot repeated word for word the testimony he had offered with the jury out in the afternoon:

—That he and Deputy Blunt had gone to the doctor's home to arrest him, that Mrs. Dreher and the two daughters were present, that Dr. Dreher told of expecting them.

—That Dr. Dreher took the sheriff and his deputy into his bedroom where he declared "I knew you would come and get me. This is hell. That man has led me a life of hell. I have feared for my life all the time. He kept my home in darkness."

—That Dr. Dreher had said Jim Beadle killed LeBoeuf. "I didn't kill him." he added that Beadle did it "out of friendship for me," and that he had not paid Beadle to do it.

During all of this, Ada sat, not looking at the witness, not looking at the judge, not looking at the jury, her eyes fixed somewhere in the distance, occasionally grimacing as in pain as the gory details were recounted. Once she brought her hands to her face as if to block out the scene which seemingly passed in front of her.

Pecot concluded his testimony and Vuillemot took the stand himself to tell how he had been summoned to Morgan City to accompany Dreher back to Franklin. The district attorney told how Dreher had been fearful of an attack upon him enroute out of Morgan City and Berwick, of his comments during the ride after first noting: "You are the district attorney. I'll have to be careful how I talk." Vuillemot said Dreher claimed that Beadle "cut it [the body] open. I didn't have the heart to turn around and see him do it."

There was a long legal wrangle over the admissibility of Ada LeBoeuf's confessions. Sheriff Pecot told his story, then Chief of Police Louis Blakeman, and Vuillemot. In their wake came Gladstone Allen, the stenographer who had taken Ada's confession in jail in Franklin. Allen said there were no threats, promises, acts of violence, or intimidation that would make the confessions inadmissible.

Parkerson argued against admitting Ada's confessions, first the oral and then the written, saying that she had been advised to turn state's evidence on the grounds that things would go easier for her if she did. He stressed what a shock it must have been to her at being arrested for her husband's murder. But additionally, he said, the confessions contained no incriminating information that had a bearing on the case.

L. O. Pecot picked up for the defense from there. A statement which denied guilt certainly could not be considered a confession, he insisted.

But Judge Simon overruled the defense. "This may or may not be a confession, but I am firmly convinced it is an incriminating statement. This was a secret homicide and anything tending to bring it to light within the law should be admitted. It is for the jury to decide the worth of this statement. I find that it was obtained freely and voluntarily on the part of the defendant."

Before the night session adjourned the confessions had been sent to the jury, but included only Ada's written statement.

So it stood. The state had:

—Beadle's confession that Dr. Dreher killed LeBoeuf,
—Ada's written confession,
—Dr. Dreher's confession.
And, of course, Ada's confession to the newspapers.

12

Wednesday, August 3, 1927

The trapper felt trapped. As court resumed Wednesday, Jim Beadle bolted from his alliance with Ada and the doctor, "confessing" to a role in the murder, but fingering Dr. Dreher as the one who pulled the trigger. His offer to testify for the prosecution was rejected.

Martha Dalrymple of the *New Orleans Item*, one of three reporters who interviewed Ada in her cell and ruled out of the courtroom as a defense witness Tuesday, was allowed back when Parkerson compromised that she not be allowed to talk to the defendants. Meigs Frost of the *New Orleans States* was excused and allowed to go home after his minor attack of appendicitis the previous day.

"Is Gwen Bristow [the *Times-Picayune* reporter and the third interviewer] in the courtroom?" asked Vuillemot, moving to exclude her from the rule. The defense objected. It would not consent unless she promised not to question the defendants further. But where was she?

"The young lady's locked up in jail, she can't come to the courtroom," said Sheriff Pecot.

"What's she in jail for?"

Chief Justice O'Niell, from the chair he had occupied as a spectator since the trial began, leaned over to another reporter for the *Times-Picayune*, and offered to get her out with a writ of habeas corpus.

"It would have to be a mandamus," replied the reporter, "She insisted on going to jail, wanted to know how it felt."

Beadle's attorney called their first witness, John Bigler, who said he had seen LeBoeuf and his wife about 7:30 p.m. the night of July 1 riding in two separate boats in the vicinity of Emory Bonner's house near the Negro school and behind the church where the murder allegedly was committed. He said he heard two shots about 8:30 apparently from a shotgun and coming from the direction of the school. On cross examination, he said he had not seen either Dr. Dreher or Beadle that night.

Edville Plesalla, who had been tendered to the state as a witness, corroborated Bigler's account, but said he had heard no shots. "I saw her come back, but not him." That was about 10 o'clock, he said.

Stealthily, Himel approached the real question on which Beadle's defense rested.

"Did you ever see Dr. Dreher meet Mrs. LeBoeuf in Morgan City?"

Parkerson jumped to his feet. "The question is irrelevant and incompetent. What is Mr. Himel seeking to prove?"

"The enmity of Dr. Dreher for Jim LeBoeuf—who had an interest in killing LeBoeuf—the question is important as far as Jim Beadle is concerned in that it is designed to show motive."

Counsel for Ada and Dr. Dreher held that since all the defendants were jointly charged, testimony as to motive was not admissible except so far as it concerned Beadle. Himel countered that this was only when one of the co-defendants was on the stand and could not possibly apply to the cross-examination of a state's witness. It is always admissible, he added, for one defendant to show who had a motive for killing the victim.

Cross-examination by counsel for one defendant, Judge Simon ruled, could not be limited to anything, except that all testimony must have a bearing on the defense of the victim.

Plesalla was allowed to continue. Had he ever seen the defendants together elsewhere?

"I saw Dr. Dreher back of the mud flat. I saw him first and then three or four minutes later, I saw her. He went into a Negro house by the cotton switch [on the railroad] and pretty soon she came along and went in, too. They came out about twenty-five minutes later. That was a month ago. I never saw them together before then."

There, now, it was on record, all these whisperings as to trysts between Ada and the Doc, gossip as to assignations between the two. Himel cross-examined Ada and Dr. Dreher. If the state would not pursue this to prove its case, Beadle's attorney had no such compunctions.

Next, the state hauled into the courtroom the infamous green pirogue from which either Dreher or Beadle was alleged to have fired the fatal shots—the angle irons, the bullet taken from the body, Beadle's brown-stained knife. Ada broke and wept as the jury examined the pirogue.

The state rested its case following an afternoon recess, and now with the jury back in the box, the Beadle confession, read in the jury's absence, was accepted and it became two to one—Ada and Dr. Dreher asserting that Beadle fired the shots, Beadle denying it and pointing the finger at the doctor.

When court resumed at nightfall attention centered again on Ada when her attorney called her to testify in her own behalf.

Parkerson began with routine questions: She lived in Morgan City? How many children did she have? Were they the same as appeared in court with her?

Parkerson recited the charge against her. Did she know Dr. Dreher? Yes.

"Did you have any conversation with your husband about July 1?"

"I did."

"Did it relate to Dr. Dreher?"

"It did. On the first of July I had my little girl take a note to Dr. Dreher. I told Dr. Dreher my husband had agreed to meet him on Lake Palourde, and they could be friends again."

"Have you ever been boatriding with your husband?"

"Yes. We went right often."

"Mrs. LeBoeuf, I'll show you a document. Is that your handwriting?"

"Yes, sir."

A sheet of note paper was circulated around the courtroom. Ada looked on serenely, her brows raised. On occasion she almost had a smirk on her face. Dr. and Mrs. Dreher had serious expressions, apparently prepared for almost anything, but seemingly confident.

"Mrs. LeBoeuf, examine this document. Is it the note written by you to Dr. Dreher on or about July 1?"

"It is."

"I notice the heading is Friday. Was the first of July on a Friday?"

"Yes, sir."

Handing the document to her, Parkerson continued. "I ask you to read the note."

Her hand trembled ever so slightly as she took the note from the attorney. Her voice was strong and without emotion as she read:

"Friday. Dear Doctor: Jim and me will go boat riding tonight on the lake. I talked to him and I believe he will treat you friendly, so meet us tonight and fix this up friendly and we will be friends. I am tired of living this way hearing Jim say he is going to kill both of us. As ever, Ada."

Again her hand trembled ever so slightly as she handed the note back to Parkerson, giving the appearance of a plain, dull woman, her lips tightly compressed as though she was afraid if she opened them, a stream of unwanted denials would come swirling out of her mouth. In front of her sat Jim Beadle, glaring at her through squinting eyes.

"Mrs. LeBoeuf, what time of day did you write this?"

"Between 2:30 and 3 o'clock."

"Did you go boat riding?"

"Yes, about 7:30. We went to Emory Bonner's and sat around about ten minutes and Jim said 'Let's go, Mama," and we left in separate boats became we had always gone riding that way.

"What kind of boats were they, pirogues?"

"No. Just boats."

"What happened then?"

"My husband asked Johnny Bilger the way to Lake Palourde and we paddled out the old shell road. We had gone about 50 feet on our way back when another boat approached us. The other boat came up about four feet. The doctor said, 'Is that you Jim?' My husband said, "Yes. Who is that?' The doctor said, 'This is me. This is Doc. Your wife told me to meet you her and we would be friends again.' 'Friends, hell,' my husband said. 'You have that damned Beadle with you' and fired a shot. Two shots came from the other boat and my husband fell dead."

"Who fired those shots?"

"Jim Beadle, I judged. Two people were in the other boat, Dr. Dreher and Jim Beadle. Jim LeBoeuf fired the first shot, Jim Beadle the other two."

"Three shots?"

"I was nervous and the doctor said, 'My God, Jim, look what you have done!" Jim said 'Well you can't blame me, he fired first.' Then Jim said. 'We must take this body in to the officers.'"

"What became of you?"

"I started for town, Mr. Beadle and the doctor showing me the way. When we got into town, he said 'Now, can you see your way?'"

Ada was like a shy schoolgirl, occasionally smirking, but otherwise reciting her story with no show of emotion.

"Did you anticipate any trouble?"

"No, sir."

Ada said she had sent another note to Dr. Dreher by way of Rosalie Hebert, a confidante and sometime dressmaker, and testified she had been ill about three years.

With this, Parkerson surrendered the witness to District Attorney Vuillemot.

Ada bristled in her first replies to his questions about the death tryst note. She remembered every word of the note, including her misspelling of the word "meet" as "meat."

Vuillemot's questions brought a steady barrage of objections from the defense, but he plowed on, Ada sometimes raising her eyebrows, but stony faced, replying. On occasion, she contradicted the district attorney, a spark of fire in her voice, but otherwise restrained.

Her voice became shrill, almost instantly lowered, during a sharp examination as to the etiquette of appointments.

"Dr. Dreher could have come to your house to make friends with your husband, could he not?"

"Yes, but Jim kept that loaded rifle in the house and the Doctor knew it." her voice almost became a whisper, hardly heard at the press desk.

Vuillemot now turned to the anonymous note to Mrs. Dreher which was shown to Ada's husband and which began the enmity between the two men. Ada admitted meeting with Dr. Dreher "on the sly."

Her confession was not the same as her testimony, she said, because she was not under oath when the confession was taken by the sheriff and the district attorney.

She described her husband's clothing the night of his death, and Vuillemot turned his questions back to the death scene.

"How many times did you holler?"

"I don't know."

"Very loud?"

"Not so very."

"All the time you were coming in with Dreher and Beadle, where was the body?"

"In the boat."

"Living or dead?"

"Dead, I think."

"You had seen your husband's dead body, you came back to town and met your brother and told him that your husband was waiting at the corner? You knew he was dead?"

"Yes."

"Your lawful husband?"

"Yes."

"The father of your four children, is that right?"

"Yes."

"And you told your brother that he was alive and waiting for you at the corner, is that right?"

"Yes."

Now, Vuillemot read her the statement he said she made in the reception room of the parish jail shortly after her arrest. It differed from the statements she had made on the witness stand.

"Did you make that statement?"

"Yes. But it was not under oath."

Ada was beginning to show the strain. Her voice grew more and more difficult to hear, almost a drone. Vuillemot continued to probe the difference between the statement and Ada's testimony from the witness box. She told him she was weary and nervous when she had made the statement.

"Were you so weary and nervous that you did not know the difference between right and wrong?" The words were almost a snarl.

"No," she replied between clenched lips.

The district attorney changed his tactics, apparently sensing an adverse reaction on jurors. He was almost pleasant as he continued to twist and turn from testimony to statement, worrying the differences as a dog thrashing about with an old rag, shaking it until it began to unravel—her conversation with Emory Bonner, the statement she made to Dreher that her husband was "gone," the body, the cemetery—had she not said the body at the undertaker was not that of her husband?

"You said in that former statement, 'I did not tell anyone because if I had they might have put two and two together and said he did it.' Did you say that?"

"Yes."

"Whom did you mean by 'he'?"

"Dr. Dreher."

"To whom did you mention the fact that you and Dr. Dreher and your husband were going to have a friendly meeting on Lake Palourde?"

"Nobody."

"Why were you afraid people would blame him if nobody knew he had been there? Were you trying to protect him?"

"No."

"Then why were you afraid he would be blamed?"

"Because Jim had threatened the doctor's life."

"Did you hear him make threats?"

"No."

"Then how did you know he did?"

"He threatened him in his office."

"But you never did hear him threaten the doctor?"

"Only that night."

"In those words you have quoted?"

"Yes."

"And that was the first time you had heard him?"

"Yes."

"How far were you from Jim LeBoeuf when he was shot?"

"About twelve feet."

"Did you see him carry that pistol?"

"No."

"And you don't know when he got it?"

"No. I saw him make a gesture like this and get a pistol."

At length, Vuillemot stopped. "Are you tired? Do you want to stop?"

"No." In truth, Ada was thinking that it would be best to let the district attorney run his skein and perhaps end this torture.

"As the court will adjourn at 11, I suggest the witness be allowed to take her seat as the lines of examination I am about to take will be rather lengthy," Vuillemot said.

Ada seemed to wilt before mustering the strength to return to her chair. It had been the most tiring day of the trial, certainly the most telling.

13

Thursday, August 3, 1927

Ada tossed and turned on her narrow jail house cot, restless until dropping off to sleep a couple of hours before dawn. Downstairs the Doc was equally agitated, wondering whether Ada could stand up under another day of grueling testimony equal to the day past. Beadle slept soundly, snoring loudly, the sound reverberating against the smooth-plastered masonry walls and echoing in the dark.

And all too soon, they were back in front of the jury, Judge Simon, the staring faces of spectators, and the relentless interrogation of the state's attorneys.

The white walls of the courtroom seemed as spotlights beaming in Ada's face as she resumed her seat on the witness stand. Necks craned so as to catch every agony of the witness. There were muffled whispers, capped with a few giggles. About what? she thought. This is serious business.

In her soft but dark blue voile over navy silk, Ada appeared nervous but composed. The blue was offset by an ecru lace collar serving only to accentuate the pallor of her face. Her broad Panama hat cast dark shadows under her eyes. She sat, her head held high, staring at the district attorney or the wall beyond the spectators, at her own attorneys, perhaps an occasional glance at the jury, although she normally averted any eye contact with the twelve men who would decide her fate.

In front of Ada sat Mrs. Husband. As usual, she wept openly. It was not lost on the jury. With her was her daughter, Mrs. Ben Beadle, sister-in-law of Jim Beadle and a sister of Jim LeBoeuf.

The district attorney's first question was with regard to the death tryst note.

"How did you get that note into your possession again?"

"Mr. Parkerson gave it to me last night," she replied. She spoke mostly moving her upper lip as though fearful to open her jaws.

Vuillemot led the questions back to Ada's version of what happened the night of the murder, and Ada picked up the threads of testimony from the night before.

"We had supper about 5:30 Friday night. I rang up the doctor to tell him where to meet us. He got my note earlier, about 3:30."

Jim LeBoeuf was the one who selected Lake Palourde as the rendezvous, she said, and it was he who identified the two adjoining lakes as Palourde and Flat. She said she noticed no difference between the lakes and the passes, making the round trip in three hours, just as she had told the reporters in her jail house "confession." (Many spectators knew that it took a strong paddler at least four hours and at times the current was almost a millrace.)

Vuillemot continued questioning along this line, but designed to show that the killing occurred back of the Negro schoolhouse as at first testified and that Ada was lying the day before.

"Why did you, in your confession, say 'Where do you want to go?' if the appointment for a meeting was already made?"

"I didn't ask him that," Ada shot back hotly, and added in a strained voice, "I suppose I wasn't thinking just at that time when I said that."

"Didn't you mean such and such a statement or do you regret having said it?"

"I do regret it."

"You say in your confession that your husband suggested going 'boat riding.' Is that correct?"

"Yes, that is correct."

"Yet you testified that he never made any such statement."

In a voice that was weakening and slightly husky, Ada answered that he never "suggested we go boat riding." She said what he actually said was "Come on, let's go for our ride."

Vuillemot continued to hammer at discrepancies between Ada's confession and her testimony, and she was showing the strain. At what he considered might me a breaking point, Parkerson would object, giving her time to compose herself.

All the while, Parkerson sat at Ada's elbow between her and the jury. Blanchard, Beadle's attorney, objected to this arrangement, and asked if Parkerson was in their way.

"I never in my life saw a lawyer sitting next to the witness during cross-examination," agreed Vuillemot. "I ask that Mr. Parkerson be relegated back to his seat where he belongs."

After a volley between attorneys, Vuillemot continued, "Didn't you make a statement that as soon as your husband was shot, you turned around and came home?"

"Yes."

"Didn't you confess that you told Dr. Dreher you didn't tell anyone Jim LeBoeuf had been shot because they might put two and two together and accuse him? What do you mean by that?"

"I'm not quite sure. I thought they would bring the body back to town and report the killing themselves. That is why I thought people would put two and two together."

The noon recess interrupted the torturous testimony, and only a few trivial questions followed when court resumed in the afternoon.

Now it was the turn of Beadle's attorney to cross-examine as to conspiracy, credibility, and motive. Himel asked Judge Simon to instruct the jury that nothing one witness said could be construed legally either to convict or acquit another. Simon said he would do so at the appropriate time.

But had a defendant the right to cross-examine a co-defendant? No, argued Parkerson, because nothing one defendant said could be applied to another.

"If Mr. Beadle's counsel will admit joining hands with the state, we will waive our objection to their cross-examining our client," Attorney Pecot added.

"I do not believe the state has gone far enough into motive for this serious, brutal, horrible crime," Blanchard countered. "We want to take no chances as far as Jim Beadle is concerned. We want to show who had reason to want Jim LeBoeuf to disappear, and who did not."

"Jim Beadle was shoulder to shoulder with his co-defendants for weeks and while the jury was being selected," Pecot charged. "Now he has ducked, turned turtle, like Judas Iscariot, upon his co-defendants. The burden of proof is upon the state, not upon the defendants. The counsel for the co-defendant has been given the right to rebut our testimony, but I object to this defendant's private life being gone into, dragged through the gutters of Morgan City for the alleged purpose of proving a motive for this crime."

Judge Simon said that because separation of interests came too late in the proceedings for severance of trial, and since the case had become one of antagonistic defense, each group seeking to incriminate the other, he would permit Blanchard to cross-examine as to credibility, commission, or motive for the crime, or conspiracy.

Blanchard moved that Ada write an exact copy of the "death tryst" note signed "as ever, Ada." Then he asked that she diagram the relative positions of the boats at the time the shots were fired.

Parkerson, Pecot, and Walker continued objections throughout Blanchard's questioning, until Simon, noting the time consumed, asked that henceforth only one attorney enter an objection at a time.

Blanchard resumed his cross-examination of the witness. "Mrs. LeBoeuf, how many shots were fired when your husband was killed?"

"There were three shots fired—my husband fired the first, and Mr. Beadle fired the other two."

"When you made your confession to the district attorney were you represented by a lawyer?"

"No."

"How long after did you employ an attorney?"

"I don't remember. I think on Wednesday of the next week."

"How many conferences did you have with these lawyers, Mr. Beadle, and Dr. Dreher? Is it true that you had several conferences with them?"

"Yes."

It was now mid-afternoon and Ada was finally released from the stand. Sam Blum of Morgan City was called. He was a justice of the peace, and said he had gone to Dr. Dreher's office at the request of Parkerson and L. O. Pecot to conduct a search. He said Pecot found a note in a prescription envelope among other papers in the doctor's desk drawer.

"Is this the envelope?"

"I dare say it is." It contained a note, he said, which Parkerson and Pecot tried to read aloud "and got hung up on some of the words."

"Look at this document and state whether it appears to be the document found."

"I can hardly make this out but I remember ycu saying something about 'friendly.' I didn't read it."

Blum answered a series of questions, all aimed at the good reputation Dr. Dreher enjoyed in the community.

Vuillemot cross-examined Blum. Could he testify that the document that had been shown by the defense was the same as that discovered in the doctor's desk?

"No."

"How do you know? Is the wording different?"

"I don't think so, but I didn't read it. I only heard part of it read."

Blum refused to say positively that the document had been handed to him to identify was the note Parkerson and Pecot had discovered in the doctor's desk.

"All you know is that you saw Mr. Parkerson and Mr. Pecot find a note?"

"Yes."

A number of witnesses were called by the defense, each reciting a litany as to Dr. Dreher's impeccable character. The district attorney did not cross-examine any of them. Vuillemot said they could bring a hundred, all saying the same thing.

Attorneys for both sides were as appreciative as witnesses, assuredly the defendants, when Judge Simon announced that he would not hold a night session because the Dreher defense, which would continue, was expected to require considerable time.

14

Friday, August 4, 1927

There he was, the center of attention at last, dressed in an old pale blue Spanish linen suit, a dark blue tie with white circles against his white shirt, taking the oath with his hand on a tiny Bible, before taking his seat on the witness stand.

His face looked drawn and pale, and he explained that he was totally blind in his right eye—he had been for the past four years, the result of a blood clot on the optic nerve. The one good eye never left his attorney as he answered routine question in a steady voice—he had three children, liked to hunt and fish all his life and owned three shotguns and a rifle, as well as two skiffs. The green pirogue was built by Beadle with lumber the doctor supplied.

His voice was clearly audible in his answers, although a rather colorless monotone. Mrs. Dreher was absent this day. He was alone except for his son, Ted, and nephew Eugene. The doctor nervously fingered his glasses on his knee. In front of him, Ada turned her face away as he spoke, and seemed trying not to listen.

The doctor began his version of what had happened:

"On the first of July I had a letter from Mrs. LeBoeuf about half past three telling me her husband had agreed to meet me on the lake and clear up all this foolishness in a friendly way. It wasn't in an envelope but was wrapped up in a piece of newspaper. I put it into an envelope and put it into a desk drawer in my office till I had a chance to answer it."

"Is this the note?" Parkerson asked.

"Yes."

"Did you have any other communication with Mrs. LeBoeuf?"

"No. I was busy that afternoon and had no chance to answer her note. Later she called me up."

"What did you say?"

"She mentioned the note and asked if I were going out there or not. She said she was tired of all this fuss and wanted to get things settled."

"You were not on friendly terms with Jim LeBoeuf?"

"No, sir, not at that time."

"After receiving the note and the telephone call, did you do anything?"

"Yes, about 6 I went to Jim Beadle's house. He was sitting on the gallery, and I went up and told him I got the note from Mrs. LeBoeuf and that she wanted a friendly meeting and could he take me out. He said 'Yes." He said the water was high and that we would have trouble getting the pirogue to where the deep water is, so we had better take it over now. We took the pirogue out to where the water was deep enough, on the side of the car, over by the colored schoolhouse. We tied the boat there to . . . I don't know what . . . what we tied it to."

"I took Beadle on home and told him I would be back for him later. Then I made some calls. After I was finished I went back to Jim Beadle's house. He was sitting on the gallery and I said, 'Jim, are you ready?' and he said 'Yes' and got up to go into the house to get his hat and when he came out, he had a gun. I said, 'Jim, what do you want with a gun?' He said 'Times are hard and we might see an alligator and that might mean two or three dollars to me for its hide.'"

"Were you armed?"

"No, I didn't have nothing."

A number of trivial questions followed. The trip started about 7:45, it was just getting dark, they made no attempt to conceal their movements, passing any number of people, and went to the corner of the last pass from Lake Palourde.

"On this occasion did you meet anyone?"

"Well, we met Mr. and Mrs. LeBoeuf out there."

"How were Mr. and Mrs. LeBoeuf riding at the time you met them . . . were they in separate boats or the same boat?"

"In separate boats."

"Was Mrs. LeBoeuf's boat in front or was she behind?"

"She was about 15 feet behind."

As she was brought into the testimony, Ada began to cry, gun shy from the day before, as if she were afraid any moment someone would point a finger accusingly at her and say, "She did it."

Instead, the testimony continued: "Doctor, tell the jury what happened that night, just exactly what was said by you, Mr. Beadle, and Mrs. LeBoeuf."

"Do you want me to tell you what was said, no matter if it was cuss words or not?"

"Give the exact words used."

"Well, when we got pretty close, I said, 'Hello, is that you, Jim?' and he said, 'Yes, who is that?' I said, 'It's me, Doc. I got a message from your wife this afternoon that we were to meet on the lake and talk over this foolishness and be friends.' He said, 'Friends, God damn, no! You know I told you if you ever spoke to me again I would kill you—and there is that—Beadle, too. I got the pair of you just where I want you now.'"

He paused and Parkerson prompted him "Where was Jim Beadle at this time?"

"He had been rowing but he had let his oars loose, thinking we would talk awhile and squatted or sat down in the boat."

"Where was the gun?"

"It was lying along the edge of the pirogue with the stock down. I was sitting up front and Beadle was in back."

"Then what happened?"

"When he said, 'I got you just where I want you' he made a shot. Then, just at that instant, Beadle grabbed the gun and made two shots, and LeBoeuf fell in the pirogue."

He said Mrs. LeBoeuf was still 12 or 15 feet away.

"I said, 'Oh my God.' Jim said, 'We're in a hell of a fix, ain't we?' I said, 'What are we going to do?' Jim said, 'He made the shot and there wasn't anything else to do but to shoot him.'" Mrs. LeBoeuf began to cry. Then we were all to pieces and didn't know what to do, and we talked the thing over."

"Who talked the thing over?"

"Jim and I."

"Did Mrs. LeBoeuf take any part in the conversation?"

"No, she was crying. I said, 'Jim, what in the world are we going to do?' and Jim said, "Doc, we're in a hell of a fix and the best thing we can do since the man was killed in self defense is take him into town and turn him over to the authorities. Mrs. LeBoeuf was crying and carrying on and said she was in a hurry to get home."

"We went with her until she saw the lights of the town. When we got there I asked her if she could go back alone and she said 'yes.' So she left."

"Did either of you say anything to her at the time she left you?"

"We told her not to do anything about it. Not to say anything about it until she heard from us.

"We sat there a little while and decided the best thing to do was to take him in and turn him over to the authorities, but if we did that we would all be put in jail.

"Then we thought we would leave the body in the boat, but we decided that in a day or two somebody would come along and find him and everybody saw us go out there and we would be accused of it anyhow.

"Mr. Beadle said that he thought the best thing would be to bury the body in the lake. He said, 'I'll fix him so that nobody will ever find him.'

He said he knew where there was some iron and suggested that we get them and weigh him down."

He had nothing to do with attaching the irons to the body, Dreher said.

"Then we went back into the lake. Jim pulled the boat up to where he could reach the body, and after he tied the irons on, he said, 'Well, there ain't anything to do but sink his body in the lake. I suppose a man's just like a deer. If a deer sinks, in just a couple of hours gas forms in the stomach and the body rises. I guess I better cut his stomach open so the body won't rise up.' He slit the stomach open. While he slit it, I turned my head and didn't see how he did it."

At this gruesome point in testimony, court recessed for lunch.

Ada, her face streaked with tears was led from the courtroom, back to her cell. She could not touch her food. Nor could many others who had heard the ghastly details recounted by Dr. Dreher. Judge Simon, who earlier had ordered his lunch sent in to this chambers, returned the food uneaten.

It was different with the spectators who brought their sandwiches and thermos bottles from home. Without leaving their seats, fearful others would take their place, they rustled their paper bags and the odor of warm lunch meat filled the room as they devoured their lunches.

The doctor returned to the stand after the recess, and Himel, one of Beadle's volunteer attorneys, began to question him. Parkerson objected and was overruled. Himel started over.

What, he asked were the reasons for Dreher's troubles with Jim LeBoeuf? Dreher told of the poison pen letters that Mrs. Dreher had shown to LeBoeuf.

"Jim LeBoeuf told me he would rather his wife wouldn't come to my office anymore," Dreher said. "He said he would kill me if he ever caught me speaking to his wife or any member of his family. He went to my house one evening and my wife saw him as I was not at home. My wife told me Jim had been there and talking about that letter business—that he came with the express purpose of killing me, but that since he had talked it over with her, he had agreed to burn the letters up and drop the whole affair."

"Did Jim LeBoeuf ever ask you to come to his home to ask you about all this?"

"Yes, but I wouldn't go. I was afraid he was laying a trap. Mrs. LeBoeuf told me it was a good thing I didn't come because he had brought his rifle downstairs and laid it on the piano in the parlor. Jim used to carry his rifle about in the car nearly all the time."

"Then, for two years you lived in mortal fear of your life from this man?"

"Yes. I used to keep my room in my house dark for fear he'd see me and take a shot, especially when my folks were away. They went away at the beginning of the high water, and I never turned on my bedroom light while they were gone."

There were many instances when he believed LeBoeuf attempted to take his life, Dreher said, particularly frequent in recent months. He had not spoken to LeBoeuf the whole week prior to July 1, he said.

"Why did you say 'Is that you, Jim' on Lake Palourde that night?" Himel asked.

"Well, I simply wanted to make sure it was. It was nearly dark."

"Why did you have to go way out on Lake Palourde for a friendly chat with Jim LeBoeuf?"

"That was his proposal."

"In the note introduced as evidence there is no place on Lake Palourde mentioned as a meeting place. How did you know where to find Mr. and Mrs. LeBoeuf?"

"She told me in the telephone conversation that afternoon that she was going down the shell road."

"But you just expected to paddle around until you found her?"

"Well, yes."

That brought a titter from the packed gallery. The audience obviously did not believe the doctor's story.

It now was Vuillemot's turn to cross-examine, and Dreher again described the trip to Lake Palourde, this time without any show of nervousness. He was accurate as to direction, except that when the district attorney described the latitude and longitude of one or two of the places with which he was concerned, Dreher grew exasperated. He knew the country as a hunter and a fisherman, not as a student of degrees and minutes, he asserted.

"Where did Mrs. LeBoeuf say she would meet you?"

"On the lake at the end of the shell road. We naturally thought that, instead of going out into the middle of the lake, she and Jim would paddle around by the shore."

Vuillemot had more questions about locality, then asked, "How far were you from the six-foot ditch?"

"I don't know. I've never measured the distances there."

"More than a mile?"

"Yes."

"How do you know? You said you never measured the distance."

"But that's just ordinary common sense. I can approximate distances that well."

A few more questions and the district attorney asked where the other notes were. Dr. Dreher said he had thrown them away.

"Then why did you keep this last note?"

"Because I hadn't had time to answer it. I had just gotten it that afternoon."

He said he could not say whether he had met Mr. and Mrs. LeBoeuf in the St. Mary portion of the lake or in St. Martin Parish, because he wasn't sure. Then, Vuillemot asked him to read aloud the note. He did, stumbling over a couple of words. He read, however, "Jim and I" instead of "Jim and me" as the note actually read.

"Why did you correct the grammar?" Vuillemot asked.

"It was only natural," Dreher answered wearily.

Vuillemot decided he had learned all he could from the witness and tendered him back to the court.

It had been a long day and both sides agreed to call an end to it.

The next one belonged to Beadle.

15

Saturday, August 6, 1927

Alice Lovell Beadle sat timid, frail, but unfrightened in her often-laundered brownish and distinctively housewifely homemade dress, awaiting the questions posed to her by her husband's attorney.

She did not look at the lawyers, but confidently at the jurors, a pretty little woman who looked not much older than her only daughter, Irene, who was 20. She sat briskly waving a woven straw fan, perhaps the only sign of nervousness she would show on the stand.

Ada, in front of the witness, could not bear to engage her in eye contact, keeping her head lowered and her eyes shielded by the brim of her large hat. Her son Ernest beside her laid his hand on her shoulder, and she reached up once to slip her hand into his and lay it against her cheek.

Mrs. Beadle looked directly at the jury as she said she and Jim had seven children (only one daughter) and were of modest means. She said they didn't have much money and rented their home in Morgan City. She never described themselves as poor, but agreed they did have a hard time of it.

Yes, her husband had gone riding with Dr. Dreher on the night of July 1, and when the doctor came to get him that evening, Dreher had called out "Jim, bring my gun."

Daughter Irene, a golden blonde in a pink dress, followed her mother to the stand to say only that she did not know much about the circumstances of the case—but her father didn't do it. Of that she was sure.

Beadle's lawyer, Himel, next called Morgan City Police Chief Louis Blakeman, Ada's brother-in-law.

Blakeman said he had met Jim LeBoeuf about a week before the shooting. LeBoeuf hailed him "I want to see you." He quoted LeBoeuf as saying "I want you to do something for me. I wonder if you wouldn't go with me to Dr. Dreher's office. I want to notify him to quit passing in front of my house in his car trying to see my wife."

Blakeman said he objected that LeBoeuf lived on a public street, and LeBoeuf agreed Blakeman was right after all. Then, he said, LeBoeuf asked him if he had ever seen anything between his wife and Dr. Dreher, and asked him to go out Sunday morning in the park at early Mass time. He said Blakeman would see Mrs. LeBoeuf meet and talk with Dr. Dreher, that the week before he had almost caught them there. Blakeman said he would do that if he had to, but he told his brother-in-law that Dr. Dreher had come to him, too, with a complaint against LeBoeuf charging that LeBoeuf had been following him in his automobile.

"'If I ever find out that much, if even I catch him talking to my wife,'" he quoted LeBoeuf, "'I'll kill him.'" The lawman said he tried to soothe his brother-in-law, and when next he saw Dr. Dreher he warned him that LeBoeuf was "on the warpath again" and had said he was going to kill him. He said he urged LeBoeuf later to make up and settle things amicably.

"Jim was fond of his children and couldn't bear to leave his wife. He was a man of violent temper but he would cool off right away," Blakeman said. "Once, he drove Ada from the house, only to go after her and bring her home. The man was a good provider," he said.

Himel sprung a surprise with his next witness, Deputy Sheriff Gabbie Pecot. Through his testimony, Beadle's attorneys charged that Dr. Dreher and Mrs. LeBoeuf and their attorney were trying to make Beadle their goat. This did not reach the jury, however, because it came while they were out of the room.

"Jim Beadle told me he wanted another lawyer, he wasn't getting a square deal," the deputy said. "I said I would speak to the sheriff about it. Jim said they told him Sunday morning after a conference with the lawyers, 'Jim, you stick to this statement or you will hang. You say that you did the killing and the cutting and the weighting of the body and all three of you will swear that it was in self-defense and you'll go free. It's all right to hide the body provided you killed in self-defense. We'll get you free, all right.'"

The deputy added that later on Beadle heard Ada ask the doctor about a headache Beadle had been suffering. "'Pretty soon he's going to have a neck ache,'" the deputy quoted her. Shortly after came Beadle's confession to Sheriff Pecot, and then a request for his own attorneys.

The deputy's testimony was ruled out by Judge Simon who also denied a request by Parkerson to offer witnesses to disprove questions of ethical misconduct by defense counsel.

As the afternoon session began, Himel called Louis Ratcliffe, an officer of the Morgan City Police Department. He told of a call to LeBoeuf's home on a complaint that LeBoeuf was beating his wife. He said LeBoeuf told him he wanted to quit his wife, but she refused to leave. He said LeBoeuf complained that his wife would not give his children medicine, refused to cook his meals, and showed Ratcliffe a stack of dirty dishes in the kitchen.

"We close for Mr. Beadle," Himel announced quietly. That meant that Beadle would not be placed on the stand to testify.

"We did not expect this," said Defense Counsel Parkerson. "We ask for a little time, just about three minutes for a conference."

Court recessed and shortly after, the three LeBoeuf-Dreher lawyers were back. "The defendants, T. E. Dreher and Ada Bonner LeBoeuf close their case," Parkerson announced.

In rebuttal, the state called witnesses on that part of the defendant's confessions as to the scene of the crime, and the improbability of rowing through the passes as Dreher and Ada testified.

Dr. C. C. DeGravelles, the deputy coroner, said he had gone through the passes during his Red Cross relief work and said he could not have paddled against the current, and that it was impossible to make the distance between Emory Bonner's house and the last pass in three hours. But that, he agreed on cross-examination, was his opinion and he could not swear it could not be done.

Capt. Ed Fogey, who claimed to own the best pirogue in the country and was an expert paddler of 30 years experience, followed on the stand. He said it was practically impossible for even an experienced paddler to negotiate the passes.

"I couldn't paddle a square end pirogue or even a good pirogue from Emory Bonner's house to the last pass. The current is so bad a man's got no business out there."

Even on a calm night he couldn't do it, he declared. "I don't believe she can beat me paddling a boat," he said when asked whether Ada could make the trip.

As the state's last witness, Sheriff Pecot was recalled to the stand.

"Where did Ada Bonner LeBoeuf tell you, in her confession, that Jim LeBoeuf was killed?"

"Behind the colored schoolhouse in Morgan City," the sheriff said.

"Where did Dr. Dreher say it happened.?"

"Behind the colored schoolhouse in Morgan City."

"Where did Jim Beadle say it happened?"

"In the pasture behind the colored schoolhouse in Morgan City."

Closing arguments began when court reconvened for a night session.

District Attorney Vuillemot insisted that the two men and the woman should all hang for the death of Jim LeBoeuf, "hang by the neck until they are dead, dead, dead!" They were all, he said, equally guilty of the murder, and because that was the law.

"You can't do anything but hang the three," argued Vuillemot. "There was a conspiracy of three defendants to kill Jim LeBoeuf, the killing was premeditated, and the doomed man was not given the least of chances to defend himself."

Now came Beadle's attorney, Himel.

"Dr. Dreher and Ada Bonner LeBoeuf planned to take Jim LeBoeuf out and kill him, and they took him out and killed him. I plead with you to send Jim [Beadle] back to his boys, to let him raise those little boys to be good men."

Beadle's lawyers maintained that Beadle should be freed of the charges because he was guilty only of having been present at the murder, in fear and under duress, when Dr. Dreher killed Jim LeBoeuf with Ada's connivance.

Blanchard, Beadle's other attorney, argued that law is only common sense, and common sense tells that a person who is present when a crime is committed need not be guilty of that crime. The husband of many faithful years, he said, had been sacrificed on the altar of Ada's illicit love. Beadle, he said, was a victim of circumstances.

By now it was almost 11 o'clock and it remained only for attorneys for Ada and the doctor to be heard the next day, and the state in rebuttal, before the jury would receive the case.

Meanwhile, those in the courtroom were not the only ones eager for the trial to end. A spokesman for the parish estimated the trial was costing $600 a day, and though the police jury had appropriated $10,000 cost may be more—damages to the courthouse by the crowds attracted by the trial exceeded $400, and more and more chairs were being broken. Remains of 50 chairs were removed after one session alone after they collapsed under the weight of too many people standing on them to get a better view of the proceedings.

At the end of the night session, the defendants were led away, back to their lonely cells, which even in the day provoked feeling of isolation.

There were no massive iron doors to clang behind them as the entrance to the jail was a simple doorway leading into the reception room from the red exterior walls covered with Virginia Creeper, a pleasant enough impression from that one associated with prisons.

The door opened into a bare, clean, concrete-walled lobby by which one ascended to the upper floors by an iron stairway. Upstairs, an inner cell of iron grating was reminiscent of a white cage set in a white box.

On the second level, Beadle was confined to a separate cell, while the doctor was accorded the privilege of having his iron cot in the hallway, and a plain pine table. As the prisoners were led to cells, the doors clanged shut behind them, the key crunching in the lock as the jailer turned it, and leaving each to contemplate the night and their thoughts of the day, footsteps echoing down the iron stairs into an empty silence. Even the normal sounds of the free life failed to filter into this cloister after the initial noise of numerous automobiles of the courtroom spectators shifting gears, sputtering and backfiring their way homeward down the gravel streets around the courthouse. Then all was silence. At least the windows of their cells were screened to exclude the mosquitoes, and the thick jail walls and metal floors lent a barrier to the summer heat.

Downstairs, in Doc's area, jail house artists of past incarcerations had left their marks, the head of a girl, not badly drawn, labeled by the semi-literate sketcher "Dierest"; the penciled silhouette of two houseboats towed by a tug. The latter showed promise, with a good sense of line and angles.

But above everything was the intense weight of absolute silence, of aloneness, of foreboding. Tomorrow could mean freedom or the hangman's noose.

International News Service interviewed the prisoners as the trial was reaching its end.

"Up until Monday," Ada said, "I honestly thought I would go free. I didn't think they had anything on me, but they won't believe my story and the way the district attorney made me blunder, I'm afraid the jury won't believe me, either.

"I'm pretty sure they won't hang me, for I don't think they would hang a woman, but I'm afraid now they will give me life imprisonment and I'm so afraid of it."

"Oh my God, I don't know what to think," Dr. Dreher told INS. "I didn't do the killing, but I know that doesn't make any difference. I'd like to think that some day I could go back to my work and start all over with my family, but I don't expect that. I'm afraid they certainly will put me in jail for life, but oh, if they just don't hang me."

"Well, I tell you," said Beadle, "I sure thought I was a goner if I stayed with that crew. Now I just almost believe I'm going to get off free like I deserve, or anyway I just don't see how they can give me much. That is, if that crowd and that jury they picked don't knife me."

16

Monday, August 6, 1927

The defendants woke early to sounds of voices and laughter from the exterior of the courthouse as the spectators returned for yet another circus day of gawking at the prisoners, whispering behind their fans and giggling, hauling in their sandwiches and soda pop and thermos bottles, scrambling for the wooden folding chairs demarking the circular arena in which the very lives of three human beings were at stake.

Over that noise was that of workmen hammering away at new house construction. From their windows they could see the tops of the palm trees of the courthouse square, and the brilliant green of other trees shining in the sun. Doc could see the courtyard which separated the jail from the courthouse, already beginning to fill with newspaper reporters and photographers waiting to snare them for quick statements as they headed to court. From his cell windows he saw, too, the sluggish brown waters of the Teche, with small slowly moving emerald islands of water hyacinth pads accentuated by their colorful blossoms which eventually would find their way to the Atchafalaya. The proliferating water plants, snags to motor-driven water craft, were not indigenous to Louisiana; some said they were stray plants brought from the Orient and shown at the Cotton Exposition at New Orleans some years before, and loosed in the bayous, quickly adapted to Louisiana waterways.

Defense counsel Walker offered the artful dodger arguments of the case as the day's proceedings began. First, he contended that disposition of a body is not proof of intent to murder. The killing, he contended, of Jim LeBoeuf by Jim Beadle after the husband had fired on him and the doctor, as both Mrs. LeBoeuf and Dr. Dreher had testified, took place, he said, in St. Martin, not St. Mary Parish, thus not in the jurisdiction of the court. Because venue of the crime had not been proved beyond reasonable doubt, Walker said, the defendants should be freed.

The lawyer implicated the press for laying blame on the defendants. "If the papers would pay more attention to their home city, we might be able to walk the streets of New Orleans with a little more change in our pockets and with a little more safety than we do."

State attorney Isidore Gajan replied, "Dr. Dreher's statement that 'he [Beadle] shot him for me' told as clearly as anything that a conspiracy existed among Dr. Dreher, Beadle, and Ada." The latter, he said, led the victim to his death.

Eight-year-old Liberty LeBoeuf sat in her mother's lap, looking with her dark eyes in childish curiosity at the attorneys parading before her, not understanding what they said, and at the audience, not knowing why they were there and why they apparently had such animosity toward her mother. Tired, as the afternoon dragged on, she tilted her golden-haired head back against Ada's bosom and from time to time rubbed her sleepy eyes with her chubby fists, trying valiantly not to go to sleep.

Ada's mother sat beside her, and looking at Libby, her eyes welled with tears. Ever so slowly she lifted her eyes to look at Ada, and covered them with aged hands and sobbed.

As her attorneys pleaded for her life, Ada could not look at Libby, not even when the child cuddled against her as if she wanted to be rocked to sleep. A clap of thunder caused the child to start. Ada looked at the man pleading for her life, at the jury who would decide her fate, but not at Libby, not at her mother. By Ada's side, too, was her youngest son, Herman, 12, who sensed what was happening and looked on wide-eyed and solemn.

Defense counsel Pecot urged that the best of men might not remember the words of an oral confession—harking back to testimony by Sheriff Pecot relative to her earliest "confession." Further, the note introduced as evidence, in which Ada spoke of a "friendly" meeting was more to be relied upon than Sheriff Pecot's statement that Dr. Dreher had told him "You'd better get him before he gets you," he said. "Accept the testimony of witnesses who know, not those who think that thus and thus are probable," he argued.

Pecot continued, contesting the evidence of Alex Comeaux who had testified he heard two shots from the direction of the Negro school at the time the murder was said to have taken place, and recalled Ada's statement that she wasn't under oath then, "and I am under oath now." Sworn statements from the witness stand were more reliable than their first confessions, he contended.

"I plead with you, gentlemen of the jury, send Dr. Dreher and Ada Leboeuf back to their families," he said in closing.

It was only then that Ada looked down at Libby. She smoothed the child's hair, almost timidly, almost as if Libby was somebody else's little girl. She straightened Libby's dress, her fingers faltering as though she had forgotten how.

After Libby had become very tired, her grandmother whispered something to her and she dropped down from Ada's lap. Herman wiggled in his chair; he, too, was tired. Hesitating, Ada put her arms around him, holding him close. Then she told him he could go. He went down the courtroom aisle, holding Libby's hand. Ada turned her head away from the poignant scene.

After a brief recess, Parkerson took up the argument: "There is a preponderance of evidence in favor of these defendants." He was speaking only for Ada and the Doc; Beadle, of course, had his own attorneys. "And there is nothing for you to do but to give the benefit of this evidence to the accused." He characterized testimony by several state witnesses as "trivial."

"And that's all the case the state has, gentlemen, except those confessions made by the accused soon after their arrest. Without giving Mrs. LeBoeuf time to consult counsel, the district attorney brought her out of her cell and got her to give a statement. But I have looked over this statement time and time again, and I find in it nothing incriminating to Ada LeBoeuf."

The courtly defense counsel warmed to his thesis. "Ada wrote this note to Dr. Dreher under her husband's orders. Dr. Dreher did not fix the place for the meeting. Jim LeBoeuf fixed it. Jim LeBoeuf carried a pistol and went out there with murder in his heart. If Jim Beadle hadn't carried a gun that night, Jim LeBoeuf would be on trial here today for the murder of Dr. Dreher, instead of Dr. Dreher being on trial for the murder of Jim LeBoeuf.

"They will tell you what a good man Jim LeBoeuf was. But I ask you, does a good man beat his wife and kick her and make her sleep in the garage, without absolute proof of her guilt?

"I warn you, gentlemen, that even eyewitnesses cannot be absolutely trusted. Sheriff Pecot may easily be mistaken in what he said the doctor told him."

District Attorney Vuillemot closed arguments. "This case is not quite like the Gray-Snyder case [a sensational murder case then in the news]. Jim LeBoeuf was not killed by a man who wanted to enjoy his big insurance check. He was killed by a man who wanted his wife." Testimony by Ada and the Doc was "gooseberry," he stated. And there the state and defense rested their case.

Now it was the turn of Judge Simon. "Gentlemen of the jury, the crime charged against the prisoners at the bar is that of murder. A judge is not committed to assist a jury in arriving at the facts, to make comments on the facts. It is his duty to instruct the jury simply on the law.

"The jury is the sole judge of questions of fact and must consider only such facts as are legally admitted into the record of a case; statements of lawyers unsupported or irrelevant must not be considered."

The judge dwelled at length on the law of conspiracy and the definition of an abettor, both of which penalties could be assessed against several defendants. To justify the plea of self defense, he asserted, there must be a physical attack or "a hostile demonstration of such a nature as to lead to the belief, beyond a reasonable doubt, in the mind of a defendant that its purpose was to destroy life or inflict great bodily harm.

"Whatever is said by one defendant, either for or against a co-defendant, must not be considered in any way except as it applies to the person making the statement," Judge Simon instructed the jury.

He then sent the jury off to deliberate. Jurors were not long in their examination of the case. Shortly they sent word that they had arrived at a verdict after the first ballot, and three minutes later, they filed back into the courtroom, their faces solemn, funereal. The over-packed courtroom was silent as spectators strained to hear.

Dr. Dreher stood, impassive, as the jury filed in, his eyes searching for some hope in the demeanor of the jury, but finding none. Ada, too, was marble-like, her face pasty with heavy powdering. Her tongue flickered fleetingly across her lips but without even the hint of emotion.

"Gentlemen, have you reached a verdict?" asked Judge Simon, his face stern, immobile.

"We have," answered L. S. Alleman, the foreman. He held a folded piece of paper.

"Is that your verdict?"

"It is."

"Hand it to the clerk."

Clerk of Court Wilbur Kramer took the paper and handed it directly to the judge. Judge Simon's face was inscrutable as he read it and handed it back to Kramer.

Kramer read it aloud: "Dr. Thomas E. Dreher, guilty as charged. Ada LeBoeuf, guilty as charged. James Beadle, guilty without capital punishment."

There was a loud gasp from spectators. They had not expected the verdict. Simultaneously, there was a loud, piercing scream from Beadle's wife which circled the round ceiling. She and her daughter Irene had to be led assisted from the courtroom, their wails trailing them through the corridor and out on the front lawn of the courthouse. The audience sat in stunned, stony silence but there was no doubt their sympathies went out to the trapper's wife and sizable family.

Ada seemed to wilt, and was supported by her son, Ernest, who had been at her side from the beginning. He dropped his head to her shoulder and began, for the first time publicly, to sob, discarding his previous facade of strength. Herman, who had returned to the courtroom, clung to her on the other side. Niece Virginia Blakeman, seated nearby, began to weep silently.

Morgan City Police Chief Louis Blakeman, who gave strong testimony against Ada, was seated behind her. As the verdict was read, he allowed a look of horror to flash across his face. His mouth dropped open at the unexpected decision.

Equally astonished was Dr. Dreher who almost staggered as the words were intoned. He stared straight ahead, deadly serious and frightened like one of the animals he so frequently had stalked in the Atchafalaya wilderness.

"Gentlemen, is that your verdict?" Judge Simon asked.

"It is," Alleman answered.

"Poll the jury Mr. Kramer."

One by one the jury responded that this was indeed their verdict.

For all of their surprise, onlookers derived a macabre sense of satisfaction in the other two verdicts, a righteous belief that Ada and the Doc were siblings of the devil and had transgressed against James LeBoeuf, even without the horrible death of which they had been convicted.

Judge Simon gulped, but in a voice as firm and almost as calm as when he had instructed the jury, gave the final orders of the day, that the prisoners were remanded to the custody of the sheriff, that they were to be held in parish jail and returned to court on Wednesday following, at which time they would be sentenced formally.

"These defendants have been the most remarkable defendants in my 33 years experience," Chief Justice O'Niell observed to newsmen as to their conduct in public. The jurist sat through the entire trial, well aware that ultimately the case would be before his court on appeal.

And appeal there would be.

"They won't hang," a stubborn Defense Attorney Parkerson said as he walked slowly from the courtroom trailed by reporters. "I have six affidavits from men who swear that three of those jurors said they would hang Dr. Dreher and Mrs. LeBoeuf if they were selected for the jury. I didn't get these until today. I know we won't have any trouble on appeal.

"That verdict was not rendered on the evidence. It was the newspapers that did it. Those jurors didn't get their opinion from the trial. They got it from the newspapers. From the first, the public has yelled for the blood of Ada LeBoeuf and Dr. Dreher. We have fought against a hostile press, a hostile public, a hostile district attorney's office, and a hostile clerk's office.

"But I have incontestable proof that the jury was packed. Packed, I tell you! I'll fight to the limit! They won't hang."

Meanwhile, the defendants, freshly convicted, were led away to their cells. Ada walked back to the jail in shaken silence, her sons beside her.

She climbed the stairs to her cell, and denied the privileges of the runway she had received since first jailed, she was led into an inner cell.

"I'll have to lock this door, M'am," her jailer said.

"Lock it," Ada snapped at him, and turned to her two sons. Both threw their arms around her and wept. For the first time since the verdicts, Ada broke, flinging her arms around her boys, and sobbing great tearful sobs.

As he neared the jail, Doc's steps began to falter as he walked unsteadily into the inner cage to which now he was restricted as a convicted murderer, the door locked behind him, too. He sagged into the single stiff chair allowed him, his hands dropped limply between his knees, his head slumped forward on his chest.

"I didn't think thcy would do it," he moaned aloud. "I didn't think they would do it. God knows I told the truth. Oh God, how could they do it?"

Jim Beadle, his wife and daughter unrecovered from their shock at the verdict, quietly entered his cell and sat down. He said nothing. What was there to say? His life had been spared. With luck he would not have to serve long.

17

"You, Ada Bonner LeBoeuf, and you T. E. Dreher, are to be hanged by the neck until you are dead, dead, dead. And may God have mercy on your souls."

The words, in themselves, surprised no one, nor did the dignity with which the state's youngest judge pronounced them. But the public still reeled from the impact of the convictions of Ada, the Doc, and Jim Beadle, the latter given a life sentence as recommended by the jury.

Prior to passing sentence, Judge Simon denied a motion from the defense for a new trial. The defendants were fairly and impartially judged, he said. Had the defendants anything to say? he asked.

"No, sir, I have not," Dr. Dreher answered in a firm voice reminiscent of his demeanor during his testimony. Neither did Ada have any remarks.

Ada, who heretofore had said she would not cut her hair, appeared in court with a short bob. It was attractive, but its purpose, seemingly, was that she expected a long stay behind bars and shorter hair was easier to manage than long.

Immediately following sentencing, Parkerson filed notice that the defendants were taking a suspensive appeal to the Louisiana Supreme Court, returnable October 1. Until that was heard, Ada and the Doc would remain in the St. Mary jail. On Monday, Beadle would be taken to the state penitentiary to begin serving his life sentence.

Proposed testimony by J. O. Slade, that Beadle had told him in a drunken encounter near the Southern Pacific railway bridge at Morgan City that he had slain LeBoeuf, went a glimmering after he was identified by telegrams from New Orleans and Denham Springs as being a professional witness.

Slade had offered an affidavit—as had Charles H. Morgan of Meridian, Mississippi—that Beadle, who he recognized subsequently from newspaper photographs, told him that he had killed a man on the lake, but wasn't worried because if the body were to be found a doctor who had been intimate with the victim's wife would be held responsible. District Attorney Vuillemot said that if Slade showed up in Franklin he would be charged as an accessory to murder.

Parkerson withdrew motions based on Slade's proposed testimony for the defense, and also decided not to pursue allegations that three jurors had said, after being chosen, that they would hang Dr. Dreher and told friends about it. He said information about the three was hearsay and could not be proven legally. That took the wind out of the defense's sails, but not out of its rhetoric.

Furthering his remarks, Parkerson said the crowding of spectators behind the jury box, presence of the telegraph instruments in a room adjoining the courtroom, and proximity of press tables occupied by a hostile group of correspondents precluded fair trial. Parkerson bitterly attacked the press again. "No sooner did they hear about the Slade affidavit than they filed their teeth and convicted him of being a professional witness. This case was tried before court opened in the newspapers and the defendants were then and there convicted."

"If that's the case," said Vuillemot smiling, "then my conscience is clear. I haven't convicted anybody or caused anybody to be sentenced to death."

The motion for a suspensive appeal to the Louisiana Supreme Court meant that execution of the sentences could not take place until the high court ruled.

Initially, the tedium of daily jail routine was broken by visitors from home, from her attorneys preparing appeals. Ada's 38th birthday in September after the trial and before appeals was rather festive. In the morning, she received her brother-in-law, Louis Blakeman, and Ernest, Herman, and Liberty, her children, and Blakeman's children, Cora and baby Helen. Ada shared with them a chocolate cake with 38 candles in little candy rosebud holders which they brought to brighten her day. Then came James Parkerson, her attorney, and later, the Rev. John McCormick of the Franklin Methodist church.

Among visitors that day was Gwen Bristow, a *Times-Picayune* reporter who had covered the trial. She was present when jailers brought in a second cake, a fluffy white concoction with little knobs of silvered frosting and spelling out "Happy Birthday." Accompanying this was a complete dinner catered by a local restaurant—shrimp cocktail, tomato salad, friend chicken on toast, French fried potatoes, green peas, and the cake—all from the attorney who had prosecuted her. She shared the dinner with Bristow, sent half the cake to the Doc and saved a slice for Deputy Martel. Doc sent a slice to Laughing Jim, a Negro prisoner whose talent for laughing was well known in the jail. Gwen Bristow wrote of her visit, quoting Ada:

> 'I have been threatening to stop having birthdays for the last four or five years. Today is positively the last one I will acknowledge. This is my last birthday.'

> The laughter went suddenly out of her voice. Her eyes shifted to look at flickering shadows on the wall. 'My last birthday,' she repeated half under her breath.
>
> 'It is lonely,' she said wearily after her last visitors had gone. 'It is always lonely, that is the terrible part about being in prison, the part that most people don't think about . . . there are visitors, a good many of them, but when it gets dark and the jailer locks up the cell and goes away, oh the terrible hours begin. It is so silent, so dark and the hours drag forever and you are so utterly, utterly alone. You think and think. There are times when I can't sleep and I sit trying not to think, but I can't help it. It is so lonely.'

But she was not alone. More from shock that a woman should be hanged for the crime than any sympathy for Ada herself, hundreds of women in the Franklin area began to circulate petitions to the state pardon board and governor for clemency. After all, if executed she would be the first woman in Louisiana history (25th in the nation) to face the ultimate sentence.

Now, however, began the first of many days behind bars as Ada and the Doc had their hopes rise and fall with each appeal. Walter B. Hamlin and Ben Daly, two of New Orleans' foremost criminal attorneys, lodged the first appeal to the state's highest court, but it was December before arguments were heard. Because one of the justices was ill, Justice O'Niell asked a delay in order that the entire court hear the case, and it did not reappear on the court's calendar until late February 1928.

Both Ada and the Doc asked for a new trial, alleging prejudicial errors committed by Judge Simon. In particular, they alleged that Beadle's attorney was permitted to cross-examine them while they were on the witness stand. They said that after they testified, Judge Simon had instructed the jury that testimony by one co-defendant could not be used for or against other co-defendants. When Beadle's attorney later cross-examined the other two defendants for the supposed purpose of establishing motive for the killing, attorneys for both Ada and the Doc had objected.

The high court took the appeal under advisement, and did not rule until April. By a four to three decision, the justices ruled that Ada and the Doc had received a fair and impartial trial and they ordered the death sentence by Judge Simon into execution.

Defense attorneys said they would apply for a rehearing and failing that, might appeal to the U. S. Supreme Court on grounds that state law was unconstitutional in shielding women from possible inclusion on juries.

Told of the court's decision, Beadle, serving his life sentence at Angola, the state penitentiary, said to newsmen: "They'll tell the truth before they hang and then everybody will know I never had no hand in the killing." Beadle, despite the fact his hunting dogs had died of "black tongue," and whose treasured mustache was ordered by the warden to be shaved, asserted to reporters that he was not bitter toward his co-defendants.

"Oh, I could watch their hanging without batting an eye," Beadle said. "A heap calmer than I was that awful night in the boat when Dr. Dreher shot Jimmy LeBoeuf. But I can't hate them. Because I guess I don't hate anybody not even a man who'd write you something that hurts you like this."

Beadle reached inside his rough flannel shirt and withdrew a single page letter which was written purportedly by the Doc and apparently before the court's decision. "I ain't had no schooling—just picked up a little so I could send notes to the gals when I was a boy." Blushing, he handed the letter to newsmen. "Here. I guess you'd better read it."

> Dear Jim. I have often wondered if you ever thought of me sitting up here in this little cell for the last eight months after having been so unjustly dealt with. Remember, Jim, I am here because the truth was not told, and I feel that if you had a heart, or one spark of manhood, or affection in you for what I have done for you and your family, you would certainly be a man and come forward with the truth. Listen to reason and it will help us. Both kindly think and pray over this and let me hear from you. Remember, you have a just God to meet some day.

"Ain't that the beatenest thing to get from a feller you know more than 25 years? A man you've lived and hunted with—been hungry and wet together? The man that's brought your babies without no charge and knows your dogs all by name?"

Beadle predicted that before Doc was hanged he would clear him of implication in the murder. "He knows who did that shooting and a man can't go to meet his God without telling. I go to church myself—went yesterday on Easter Sunday."

Was he a church member?, a reporter inquired.

"No. I just go when I feel like it—but I know there's a God, and that He'll let me go back home to my wife before very long."

The summer was long and hot, but attorneys for the condemned pair still held hopes for clemency even though the U. S. Supreme Court refused to hear the case. That decision so depressed the Doc that he ceased to exercise in the jail corridor, although he was an avid reader of newspapers, hoping to glean a ray of hope from stories of the battle waged by their attorneys.

Ada, too, showed depression, foregoing the freshly ironed summer dresses on which she had insisted before.

Even Sheriff Pecot's nerves frayed. He had come to like and to sympathize with both of his prisoners, and his spirits rose and fell with each appeal. He tried to keep them comfortable, providing them with kegs of iced water.

Summer simmered to a bleak Thanksgiving. In November, Hamlin and Daly appealed to the state pardon board, which, by law, was composed of State Attorney General Percy Saint, trial Judge Simon, and Lieutenant Governor Paul N. Cyr. Of the three, Cyr strongly favored clemency.

Mrs. Dreher and her two daughters were present at the hearing at which the formal petition of the trial jurors was presented. Two of the jurors appeared in person; the other nine signatories said in a statement that they would have appeared except for business responsibilities. The 12th juror was said to have located out of state and could not be reached.

It was an eight-hour impassioned plea, culminating in a two to one refusal to grant a commutation of sentence, despite a petition signed by 75 percent of St. Mary Parish voters to overturn the sentence and the juror's petition that their death verdict had been influenced unduly by bitter community pressure which then existed. Another view of dissenters was that the circumstantial nature of the evidence did not justify a death sentence.

The foreman of the jury, L. S. Alleman, in a separate petition, asked the board to consider commutation to life for the sake of the children. "After long and serious deliberation, I have come to the conclusion that it would be unbecoming our present civilization in the Southland for the law to take the life of a woman as the wages of sin, no matter how terrible the sin. Such a gruesome example could serve no good purpose. Life imprisonment would be a more appropriate penalty for these two humans."

Then, there was a pervasive maudlin sympathy; the two were viewed now as star-crossed lovers, the victims of local jealousy and malice. Local sentiment could have caused Cyr, who like Justice O'Niell, was from that part of the state, to become the champion of the convicted pair.

The mood of the public seemed to sway to the side of the condemned. Mrs. Charles O'Niell, wife of the chief justice, began a feminist move among Louisiana club women seeking to save Ada and the Doc from hanging. That movement gathered steam after the pardon board denied the appeal for clemency. The urgency of their cause was accentuated when, even as the pardon board met, Governor Huey P. Long was fixing the execution date for December 21 and issuing the warrant for the execution to be carried out.

Fall had come full circle. Deciduous trees lost their leaves with the first frost, accentuating the green remnants on the live oak trees. The once verdant courthouse lawn was now a light brown. And in the air, the sweet-sour odor of burning debris from the cane harvest carried on the crisp air as the yellowish brown smoke billowed over the fields.

Ada and the Doc received that news with sobs and borderline hysteria. Hamlin begged Governor Long for a reprieve "in the name of Christian decency. It is unthinkable to send a man and woman to a horrible death on the very eve of Christmas."

Rather than cast a pall on the Christmas season with an execution, particularly one with the notoriety of this case, the governor set a new date for after the first of the new year, January 5, 1929. That threw club women in New Orleans and statewide into high gear, petitioning the pardon board which had scheduled a rehearing, to grant clemency.

The New Orleans Federation of Women's Clubs voted to send a committee to the board hearing. Mrs. A. L. Pilsbury, president, said discovery of new evidence, the petition by 11 of the 12 jurors, and dissent of three supreme court justices in the decision to deny a new trial justified clemency.

Lieutenant Governor Cyr gained the support of Attorney General Saint to call the rehearing before the pardon board, with Judge Simon vehemently opposed.

Aside from the juror's petition, and testimony by the Federation of Women's Clubs (now joined by the League of Women Voters and the New Orleans Boosters Club), the board heard from witnesses relative to discovery of a pistol in the vicinity of the slaying. One chamber had been discharged.

Joseph LeBoeuf, eldest son of the deceased, said the weapon was similar to that owned by his father. "I don't know if it is the same pistol, but it looks like the one my father owned. I found all of my father's possessions in the house, except his pistol."

Both Ada LeBoeuf and Dr. Dreher had testified in their trial that James LeBoeuf had fired the first shot from a pistol, but the weapon was never produced. The pistol now offered in evidence was found in April 1928 and was in the possession of Sheriff Pecot for several months after it was found by two crawfishermen. It was only after appeals attorney Ben Daly visited with Ada and the Doc several weeks before that the pistol came to light.

Wright Wilson, a gatekeeper at Angola, testified that he had overheard Beadle admit to the actions described by Ada and the Doc in the trial—that he killed LeBoeuf. Wilson said he told that to David Dreher, the Doc's brother, on a recent visit to Angola.

Wilson said he had borrowed a newspaper from visitors, and Beadle passed by. He said he asked Beadle if stories relative to Ada and the Doc were true. He said Beadle replied:

"Well, if I tell the truth, I'll never get out of the penitentiary."

Wilson said he did not see why, and Beadle said:

"Well, I'm the man who shot LeBoeuf. After I shot him, I put the angle bars on him and threw him in the lake. The next morning I went out and broke up LeBoeuf's boat."

Wilson said his wife had also heard Beadle's admission and could corroborate his story except that she was confined to her bed by sickness.

Emory Bonner, Ada's brother, testified his sister and Dr. Dreher did not plan to kill Ada's husband. He said LeBoeuf and his wife stopped by his wife's the night of the killing and asked him and his wife to accompany them on their boat ride.

"Did you ever tell this to the defense attorneys? he was asked.

"No, but I told it to the grand jury and to Sheriff Pecot."

"Did you testify at the trial?"

"No, but I was summoned as a state's witness and never called."

Bonner's wife corroborated her husband's testimony. She said the LeBoeufs asked them several times that night to accompany them, but the Bonners declined because they had just returned from a trip to Beaumont and the children were asleep. She never told defense attorneys about this, she said, because she didn't think it was important.

O. J. Simoneaux and Theodore Dumesnil, two of the jurors, appeared personally to ask clemency and declare that they had been influenced unduly by high feeling at the time against Ada and Doc.

There were others—Father J. J. Rousseau of Franklin, who said he felt the local people had been prejudiced against Ada because she had been painted as "a public woman." He admitted he had been prejudiced against the pair from what he had heard at first, but later had altered his view after hearing the trial. For example, he said one witness told of seeing Dr. Dreher and Mrs. LeBoeuf enter a certain Negro cabin in 1927. "I went to that house and the water marks were about three and one-half feet high. Morgan City was under water at that time."

On December 21, 1928, the pardon board reversed its earlier decision and moved to recommend clemency—Cyr and Saint for and Simon against. In his dissent, Simon said, in part:

"It is inherent in man to be always responsive to the demand of some degree of public sympathy. It is the natural milk of human kindness which flows through the veins of humans. Hence, it is but natural to find, after time has healed the wounds and the unfortunate victim forgotten, that sympathy is quickly aroused from the emotions of men and prompt to accede to the wishes of those who are interested parties, directly or indirectly.

"Hence, it is that we find jurors, who are laymen, reversing their former opinion which was reached after mature deliberation, and when fully cognizant of the duties which rest on them in regard to justice as between society and individuals over whom they are called to judge."

The free and voluntary confessions made by Dr. Dreher and Mrs. LeBoeuf, Judge Simon added, destroyed any merit to new evidence adduced at the pardon board.

The board's reversal posed a dilemma for Governor Long. If he permitted the execution to take place, he would be in defiance of the Board of Pardons. If he bowed to the will of the majority, he would have to ignore the evidence in the trial. If he followed the board's recommendation, he would be seen as yielding to pressure, especially to Cyr, or he could openly break with his political rival.

Governor Long was considered a brash new interloper into state politics, and had numerous critics among the planter aristocracy who had for some years held state power. Those critics recognized a possible means of lessening the support of a man who would condemn to death a woman—and a white woman at that. Cyr was not above political motive, either, aspiring to the office of governor at the next election. Long thus branded the pardon board's recommendation for mercy "a mockery against decency and civil order in the state."

In a statement to the *Times-Picayune* via telephone from his home in Shreveport, Long said:

> I am hoping to see something in the papers showing which one of the two tales these two murderers told is true. They swore one thing when arrested and tried. That did not work, so they come back and swear directly the opposite.
>
> About the only thing I am interested in, other than the record as formed at the trial, is a statement from these two murderers setting forth which time they were lying, or which time they were telling the truth, assuming they were telling the truth one time out of two. I would like to know what happened to cause these two murders to change their own tales.
>
> I will go into this matter again and consider it, but that is how I feel about it.

Long stood by his execution date, January 5, 1929. That infuriated Cyr who declared the governor had "double-crossed" him, that he had asked Long to leave the state (making Cyr acting governor), and this would permit him to commute the death sentences.

Thinking he had Long's agreement, Cyr motored from his home in Jeanerette, on the edge of St. Mary Parish, to the capitol. But Long had not left, and Cyr could not understand why Long declined to cross the state line into Mississippi and leave action on the pardon board's recommendation to him.

As the stalemate continued, a rumor circulated that Governor Long had been kidnapped. Cyr said he hoped the story was true. "I'd not only settle the LeBoeuf-Dreher case, but I would pardon the kidnappers," he said heatedly.

Never at a loss for words, Long shot back, praising Cyr's "wonderful, sympathetic heart. His feelings go so far that it would be hard for him to keep the penitentiary doors closed on anyone,"

The morning of January 3, Judge Simon agreed to a stay pending a hearing on application for appointment of a sanity commission to determine the lunacy of Ada and the Doc. A relatively new state law prohibited execution of insane persons, and the defense maintained that the trial had unbalanced the two defendants.

Wan and pallid, saying her rosary, Ada was carried into court on a couch. Dreher was unshaven, wearing a threadbare suit, and appearing 10 years older than when the trial began. They wept as Judge Simon declined the plea.

On the morning of January 4, 1929, Long refused again to grant clemency again. In a five thousand word statement, from which the following is excerpted, the governor said:

> I am sorry that this cup cannot pass from my lips. The pardon board's recommendation [over the protest of the trial judge] that this verdict be commuted places a responsibility on the governor which no executive would assume if he could avoid it. But only the governor is left to assume this responsibility, and to recede in the face of this circumstance would be at the expense of law enforcement and public virtue.
>
> Capital punishment is the law of the land. I am an officer sworn to enforce the law. No legislature has ever been persuaded to change that law, and even more, no legislator has ever suggested in my day that it should be changed. Until that law is repealed by the legislature no one could ask me, under my oath, to set [it] aside by an ex parte order of the governor.
>
> In this case it might be well admitted that if the penalty of capital punishment is not enforced, then there might never be such a law as this in this state.
>
> A further plea is made on behalf of the children of the condemned. It is urged that the hanging of these defendants will be a stain on the honor of those children. It may be with some of the people of this state, but in my mind it is not. The great state community should endeavor, in every way, to assist in seeing that these children are not

deprived of the advantages which they have a right to anticipate, nor of the respect which the community should afford them.

But if there is to be a stain on the family, it is the act of the murder which does it rather than the punishment, and as much as my sympathy might lead me to show consideration to any one of the score of descendants, I cannot place in jeopardy the wellbeing and life of the people of this state. To recognize such a plea would open the door of all jails and penitentiaries in this country and free every bandit that ever paraded the highways.

Finally, as to the recommendation of the pardon board for clemency, I am unable to give it the weight which I would like. The trial judge, one of the three members of the pardon board, has maintained that the law should take its course. The attorney general, also one of the members of the board, at one hearing took this position and now changes to the other side, admitting that there is practically no new evidence of any consequence to justify such a change. Only the lieutenant governor consistently recommends this commutation, and in deference to his opinion I have gone through this case, weighing every fact and circumstance; and yet, from it all I fail to find one single condition, or extenuating circumstance which would justify my thwarting the course of the law as it has prevailed in this state and this country for centuries past.

I cannot, under my oath as governor of this state, disrupt the process of the law, hold out an example that murder shall be given punishment contrary to the statutes, or that clemency should make this land one in which human life shall not have a reasonable degree of sanctity.

I therefore refuse to abide by or to follow the recommendation of the board of pardons and reject the recommendation; and I deny commutation of the sentence of death imposed upon Dr. Thomas E. Dreher and Mrs. Ada Bonner LeBoeuf.

18

Was it his wife, was it the increasing sentiment in the Teche country against the executions, was it that he had sat through most of the trial himself and doubted the result, or was it because he was politically opposed to the populist governor whose philosophy was so foreign to his own?

The slight gentlemanly chief justice had a ruddy complexion (some said it was his drinking) and a shock of unruly white hair. He had been on the high court since 1914, a staunch conservative, and thoroughly capable of acting in a most injudicious manner.

The night of January 4, the Louisiana Supreme Court met to review a defense motion for a one week stay to study Judge Simon's action refusing a sanity commission. Four justices denied the application. It was a signal for Sheriff Pecot to proceed with the executions the next day.

"Just a minute," said Justice O'Niell, drawing from his overcoat pocket two typed pages, and began to read: "Under Sections II and X of the state constitution, any judge of the Supreme Court has the right to issue a stay of execution. I issue the order and command you, Mr. Clerk, to notify Sheriff Pecot at Franklin that there can be no execution until the order can be properly carried out."

His fellow justices and court spectators sat in stunned silence as O'Niell ordered the clerk to "read the sheriff my order!" The clerk, by telephone, did so and promptly fainted. Associate Justice Brunot snatched the phone from the clerk. "Four members of this court have refused to stay the execution," he snapped at Sheriff Pecot. "Majority opinion is binding."

Justice O'Niell grabbed the receiver. "Sheriff Pecot, you will obey my order no matter what anybody else may tell you." And he hung up.

"Only one man on this court would have done that," said Justice Brunot, tight-lipped and glaring at O'Niell.

"Sir," replied the chief justice, "I will not tolerate anyone addressing me in this manner!"

Pecot did not know which way to turn. The night of January 4, Governor Long called him to issue a reprieve, but called the next morning to rescind it. The sheriff locked himself in his office, decided to take Justice

O'Niell's order, sent the hangman packing back to New Orleans, and began frantically to telephone every one in authority of whom he could think.

It posed an interesting legal question. Could one member of the supreme court circumvent the court's previous decision? Long was irate. He called the chief justice (who walked with a noticeable limp) "a crooked-legged sonofabitch." He was left with no alternative but to grant a reprieve for Ada and the Doc pending a decision by the full court on the legality of the chief justice's stay order.

A few days later, the high court met and declared O'Niell's order null and void, but allowed the defense 15 days to study their action.

In the interim, in a front page editorial, the *Times-Picayune* observed:

> Chief Justice O'Niell states that ordinarily one member of the Supreme Court will not issue an alternative writ if a majority of them think that it should not be issued. However, he goes on to point out that the Dreher-LeBoeuf case is an extraordinary one. We do not think it is, although his actions are.
>
> It is an unprecedented action for one justice to issue a writ after the court itself has refused to do so. Such a situation has not heretofore arisen and was unheard of until this time.
>
> . . . We stated that the sheriff received two orders from the court. The chief justice says this is not true. Technically, highly so, he may be correct. As a matter of fact, the majority of the court refused to grant the stay of execution and upheld the highly discretionary opinion of the trial judge. The decision was in written form, properly entered on the official record and read to the sheriff, over telephone, by the clerk. Since the stay of execution was not brought about, the sheriff's duty and orders were to proceed with the execution. The chief justice ordered the sheriff not to proceed. If the chief justice means that the majority opinion of the court did not actually state: 'Proceed with the execution,' he is correct. . . .

The newspaper noted that while the court's opinion did not contain such language, the opinion had the effect of doing so.

In reply, Justice O'Niell maintained that each justice of the supreme court, by the constitution, had authority to issue writs of habeas corpus, mandamus, certiorari, prohibition, pro warrant, and all other writs, orders, and processes subject to review of the court itself.

Ordinarily, Justice O'Niell conceded, one justice would not issue an alternative writ, but the matter before the court was not ordinary. Any member of the court, he continued, ought to exercise his authority to issue a rule if he thinks the parties are entitled to a hearing before the entire court despite a majority sentiment they were not so entitled.

On January 11, the supreme court set aside Justice O'Niell's stay of execution and reaffirmed its decision earlier (four to one) not to mandamus Judge Simon to appoint a sanity commission, but suggested a brief reprieve.

Immediately, Governor Long announced he would grant a reprieve as requested by the court to give time for orderly proceedings and further arguments by defense counsel. The governor said he would grant 15 days or until February 1. Should the court not reach its decision before then, he suggested that he might extend the death date to give himself time to review what the court decided. Meanwhile, he said, until the court declared it definitely had completed its deliberations, "I will not be further concerned with the case, nor will I talk to anyone about it nor will I read any letters or telegrams regarding it."

As days ticked by, Sheriff Pecot heard that Beadle was hysterically begging to confess to him. He and Lieutenant Governor Cyr rushed to Angola to speak with Beadle, but they were told that Governor Long had issued orders that no one could speak with the prisoner.

Cyr and Pecot raced back to the capital, hunting unsuccessfully for the governor for two days. The governor's enemies whispered that he had vowed to be the first governor to hang both a Mason and woman.

On January 18, the state supreme court, by unanimous decision, refused a 90-day stay in the execution of Ada and the Doc to permit their attorneys time to carry the fight to the U. S. Supreme Court. The court also reiterated its previous action, holding O'Niell had overstepped his authority in granting the earlier reprieve.

In a last minute scramble, defense attorneys Parkerson and Pecot failed to get the nation's highest court to grant a stay of execution. A majority of the court considering the request refused to pass on an interpretation of Louisiana law relative to the right of individual justices to issue writs. Justice O'Niell's actions, defense counsel insisted, was in accord with the state's constitution.

Anticipating such a decision, defense counsel Hamlin and Daly, having met with U. S. District Judge Wayne Borah the day before, filed a writ of habeas corpus on January 20 in his court, postponing the executions, simultaneously asking the U. S. District Court to intervene and send the case to the U. S. Circuit Court of Appeals. Daly asked Judge Borah to grant the writ until the court determined whether the defendants had received their constitutional rights for impartial trial, asserting the jury was intimidated by the courtroom crowd and that his clients were now insane and should not be hanged because new Louisiana law prohibited the hanging of the insane.

On Thursday morning, Judge Borah's office released notice to the attorneys that he had denied their application.

Later in the day, the Fifth U. S. Circuit Court of Appeals refused to interfere with the executions now rescheduled for February 1. Governor Long warned Sheriff Pecot that this time, if he had to, he would call out the state militia to enforce his order to execute Ada and Dr. Dreher.

This time there was no reprieve and Sheriff Pecot, who would not have looked forward to the death of even the hardened murderer, had no stomach for the proceedings.

All appeals had been exhausted and Sheriff Pecot finally had to tell his prisoners, Ada first.

"It's all over."

"The Court of Appeals?" she asked, her quavering voice betraying her desperation.

"Turned you down."

"The governor?" she cried.

"Says he's through," the sheriff said despondently.

"Isn't there something you can do?" Ada pleaded.

"There is nothing I can do. You must be calm."

"You always bring me bad news!" She now was like a small child throwing a tantrum, sobbing, and collapsing on her iron cot.

The Doc had cowered in his cell for weeks, but now he was the strong one, collected but resigned. "I have made my peace with God," he told Pecot. "I am innocent."

Families of the condemned had been allowed their last visits Thursday afternoon. Thursday night, Governor Long announced tersely, "The law will have to take its course."

No one would be allowed to visit the prisoners on Friday, and the execution was set to take place between noon and 3 p. m. On Friday morning, Ada and the Doc refused all breakfast, taking only milk and coffee.

The day dawned a murky gray after a cold front during the night met warm gulf air, wringing a misting rain from molten lead clouds, and leaving a deep chill even to the hardiest. It had been a sleepless night as the condemned prayed for a last minute commutation, perhaps at least, another reprieve from the courts or the governor.

Early Friday morning, Sheriff Pecot went to Ada's cell. He asked her if she would like to see and talk with the Doc.

"He's not my family doctor any more." she answered It was a resignation of the inevitable. There was no reason to prolong their agony by a leave taking, an emotional parting. They had long since said good-bye, Ada thought. In essence they had separated, became two distinct individuals, when Jim LeBoeuf's body had been found and this whole nightmare became a reality.

Now it was a matter of which of the condemned would hang first. "It will depend upon their physical conditions," Sheriff Pecot said. He had already decided he would not be the hangman, but had arranged to employ the one used by Orleans Parish.

Father J. J. Rousseau spent part of the early morning with Ada, while the Methodist minister, Rev. J. A. McCormick, prayed with the Doc in the tier of cells below.

At about 11 a. m., the Doc called for Sheriff Pecot and begged to be allowed to say farewell to Ada. The sheriff escorted the doctor to Mrs. LeBoeuf's cell. The Doc clasped her hand and looked for a brief moment into her eyes. In a firm, but unhappy voice, he said a single word: "Good-bye." And he turned and went back to his cell where he resumed his prayers.

Promptly at noon, the sheriff assembled his witnesses, other officials and a few deputies. Curious spectators were barred from the prison and all who entered were searched for cameras. Outside, a crowd slowly began to gather, and by noon an estimated 500 people gathered on the lawn in front of the jail, standing solemnly, waiting patiently. Inside, witnesses to the hanging waited in the jail dining room until they were led to the gallows area through passages freshly whitewashed.

The gallows room was a rectangular 12 by 18 feet with a metal gallows built in, all painted white, and surrounded by cells. It was spotlessly clean. The gallows trap was railed by metal pipes and on a landing leading to the cell Ada occupied.

Dr. C. M. Horton, the coroner, and Dr. F. V. Boyd took their positions and waited. Ten minutes after the courthouse clock tolled noon, the death march began for Ada. It was 15 feet from her cell before she stepped on the gallows trap.

"Oh Mother, mother." Then, "My God." and Ada continued praying softly. She was dressed in a pink housedress, once a bright pink. Blindfolded and limply leaning on the arm of Jailer Martel, Ada stepped out on the trap where the hangman began his work in jerky movements. Martel tied her skirt around her knees with string to prevent it from parachuting immodestly when she fell. The hangman lashed her ankles together.

When she stepped on the trap, Ada clasped her hands before her in prayer. Sheriff Pecot was forced to step forward and move them behind her so that the executioner could tie them there. In a high pitched, trembling voice, she implored "Don't let me hang there too long. Don't make me suffer any more than I have to."

"Oh, God. Isn't this a terrible thing? Oh God, who can do this thing? It is worse than murder itself." And then came the hood, black with white tape and fastened by a safety pin, muffling her voice, as the hangman adjusted the noose around her neck.

"Oh. Oh, that rope's too tight," said Ada, a touch of fear now showing through.

"No, it isn't tight." Martel seemed to try to reassure her.

"Yes, it is, " Ada insisted.

"You'll have to stand up now," said Martel gently moving away.

"I can't," Ada answered Martel.

"Yes you can," Martel said.

"Watch out, Arthur," Pecot warned and Martel jumped aside.

The trap was sprung and her body fell and began to swing. Father Rousseau began to intone the prayers for the dead in a low voice. Finally, Dr. Horton and Dr. Boyd stepped forward with their stethoscopes, lifting her eyelids and making other tests for life. They pronounced her dead, and after the required interval, Sheriff Pecot cut the rope. Deputies Martel and W. L. Pugh carried the body out.

The remnants of the old rope were replaced with new. Solemnly, the sheriff and Martel descended to the little white door leading to the tier of cells where the Doc waited.

He emerged and walked 20 steps, led by Sheriff Pecot and followed by Deputy Martel. Reaching the steps, he paused and looked about at the witnesses. Before hesitantly beginning the climb, he said, "Gentlemen, we don't deserve this. We are not guilty."

"Oh God in heaven, forgive them for they know not what they do," the Doc said. He repeated the prayer as he reached the platform and looked down at the witnesses. "Oh God," he said as the hangman began to secure his ankles and wrists, "two innocent souls gone to their deaths for a crime they did not commit."

He turned to Sheriff Pecot: "Mr. Charlie, ain't your heart aching?"

"Yes sir. You will soon be out of your suffering," Pecot answered.

"Is Mr. Frost [the reporter] down there? God bless you, you know we did not do this. Oh God, have mercy on me. They have killed a poor innocent woman," he sobbed. Deputy Martel stepped forward, placed the black hood over his head and secured the noose around his neck.

"That rope is too tight—do you want to choke me to death?" he protested.

Martel, intent on keeping the knot from slipping, adjusted it carefully. "I want the rope tight," Martel told him.

"Do you want me to choke—to strangle to death?" asked the Doc. "Martel, I did not think you would put the rope around my neck."

"I want to prevent your strangling," the deputy said.

The hangman moved to pull the lever. Before he did, the Doc said, "Mr. Frost, did you get my message—my last message to the world?"

"Yes," said the newsman as Dr. Dreher plummeted through the trap, faultily tied wrist cords loosening allowing his arms to swing free. The drop broke the sixth cervical vertebra, but his pulse continued to flutter for five minutes, according to Dr. Horton. After the official 20 minutes, Dr. Dreher's body was cut down.

The attending physicians insisted there had been no pain to either Ada or the Doc. It was a few minutes shy of 1 p. m.

Dr. Dreher, however, had not said his farewells in full. On Saturday, Eugene Dreher, the nephew, revealed that the doctor had entrusted a farewell message to Meigs Frost, the reporter, asking that it be given to the Associated Press. It read:

> As I sit here in my sad and lonely death cell tonight with an aching heart, I want to write my last message to the living people of this world who know something of this tragedy. I want these words to be published to the world.
>
> I wish they could be given the same prominence in the press and over the radio as our trial was given.
>
> This is my message:
>
> Poor Mrs. LeBoeuf and I go to our doom tomorrow. Two innocent souls. I may not have a chance to say anything tomorrow before they hang me. Mrs. LeBoeuf, I believe, is too sick to be able to say anything. This is why I am writing this.
>
> Neither Mrs. LeBoeuf nor I fear death. We do not fear death because we have made our peace with God and we will soon be where suffering and punishment are no more, safe at home with Jesus. Thousands know, as well as Mrs. LeBoeuf and I know, that we are innocent.
>
> Beadle killed LeBoeuf and mutilated and disposed of the body over my protests and against my wishes, saying he had done the same thing to a man years ago and nothing ever came of it.
>
> Yet, Mrs. LeBoeuf and I have been led to the slaughter like sheep. For a year and a half we have been fighting for our lives. We have fought with truth for our weapon ever since we were put on trial. We have lost. We will die game.
>
> It has been an uphill battle all the way against those who have been against us. If our lives are sacrificed, I hope it will not be all in vain. I hope that with our deaths a movement will be started to abolish capital punishment, a relic of the barbaric ages. If some movement like that grows out of the legal murder of Mrs. LeBoeuf and myself, then as Jesus died on the cross that others might live, so we too shall not have died in vain.
>
> All this story that Mrs. LeBoeuf and I were lovers is untrue. I had been the LeBoeuf's family physician for twenty years, and Jim LeBoeuf

was my best friend until that lying anonymous letter came to light. I had always prized the friendship of the LeBoeufs.

A kinder hearted or more sympathetic woman never lived than Mrs. LeBoeuf.

It is a bitter cup we have to drink, but we are going to face our God with our hearts washed clean of hatred. We were overruled on everything that might work in our favor when we fought to keep out of the record much that hurt us. God knows, and I know we both are innocent, and yet we never have had the benefit of the faintest shadow of doubt.

It is hard not to grow bitter when you stand face to face with a shameful death you have not deserved as I do tonight. I will try not to be bitter. I have forgiven those who have lied about me, and I have prayed to God to forgive them. Mrs. LeBoeuf has done the same. We can face our God with clear consciences.

The hearts of Mrs. LeBoeuf and myself are warm with gratitude to those who have befriended us in these long months of our bitter troubles. We forgive all who have misjudged us and have been hard on us. We thank our friends and all those who have assisted us.

To them, this is our last message on this earth. We are going home and will be waiting to welcome you where there is no more sorrow.

Epilogue

In his written denial of clemency, Governor Long had stated:

> It is urged (by some) that the hanging of these defendants will be a stain on the honor of (the) children. It may be with some of the people of this state, but in my mind it is not. The great state community should endeavor, in every way, to assist in seeing that these children are not deprived of the advantages which they have a right to anticipate, nor of the respect which the community should afford them.

What the governor said and what a whispering public and shamed family apparently did were not the same.

The LeBoeuf children led a hard life. In an interview with the writer, Mrs. Lynette Davis of Morgan City, great granddaughter of Ada Bonner LeBoeuf and granddaughter of Ernest LeBoeuf, told what happened to the family following the hanging.

Mrs. Davis is the daughter of Mrs. Marilyn LeBoeuf Roy (Ernest's daughter) and a grand niece of Mrs. Liberty LeBoeuf Ledet, daughter of Ada Bonner Leboeuf.

Any discussion of the murder and subsequent executions has been "taboo" in the family, Mrs. Davis said. Her grandmother never permitted any discussion of the case, and Mrs. Davis said her mother, Mrs. Roy, objected to her questioning her grandfather about it.

"It was a terrible subject in our family. My Mom grew up in the family home without it ever being mentioned. It was such a horrible thing that happened to the kids. They remember going to the courthouse and begging for their mom's life. It was so traumatic for them, and they all had their lives so affected by this that it wasn't even allowed to be discussed in the house."

Mrs. Davis continued: "Right before my grandfather died, in 1992, I sat down with him one day and asked—my Mom couldn't believe I was going to do it. I said, 'Mama, why not? He's sick and I am going to ask him questions.' And he answered them. He didn't have any problem talking to me. It was just something we were taught, never to say anything."

Ernest was seventeen when the murder happened. That, said Mrs. Davis, is the same age as her son today, "and I have tried to picture to myself what he would have to go through if that had happened to me. And I am trying to think about my grandfather, how he and my great aunt, were brought to plead for their mother's life, and that must have been so hard."

Immediately following the executions, Liberty went to live with her aunt and uncle, the Louis Blakemans, and remained a resident of Morgan City. At this writing she is recovering from heart surgery. The family did not want her to be interviewed.

Ernest married Mable Boudreaux the same month his mother was hanged, and the couple took Herman, the youngest boy to live with them. Mrs. Davis said "He was beside himself and started being a handful; nobody could control him."

Joseph and Herman moved to Galveston, Texas, never to return to Morgan City. Each married and had two children. Herman died in 1987. Joseph died in 1991.

Mrs. Davis said her mother was never told anything about the murder case and learned of it eventually from school classmates. "She didn't want us to find out about it that way, so she told us about it when I was in high school. Then she went to the library and checked out a book about Huey Long—there was an excerpt in there that she let us read. She really doesn't like to talk about it. Mama and Aunt Libby, I know, don't even discuss it to this day."

As for some of the other principals in the case:

Judge James D. Simon became a member of the Louisiana Supreme Court in 1955 and retired in 1960. He died in October, 1982.

Justice Charles O'Niell continued service on the Louisiana Supreme Court until his retirement from the bench in 1949 He died in New Orleans in March, 1951.

Walter B. Hamlin of New Orleans, appeals lawyer for Ada and Dr. Dreher, was elected to the Louisiana Supreme Court in 1958. He was the author of several books on the law and the courts. He became chief justice of the supreme court in 1972, and retired from that position in 1973. He died in New Orleans on New Year's Day, 1984.

Wayne G. Borah, who denied the appeals attorneys' application for a writ of habeas corpus, was a native of Baldwin, La., in St. Mary Parish. In 1949, after serving more than twenty years on the United States District Court for Eastern Louisiana, Judge Borah was named to the United States Fifth Circuit Court of Appeals. He retired in 1956 and died in New Orleans in February 1966.

Lieutenant Governor Paul N. Cyr took the oath of office as governor after the election of Governor Huey P. Long as U. S. senator. Long had not yet taken the oath as senator, therefore was still governor, and he declared that since Cyr had taken the oath as governor, he had vacated his office as lieutenant governor, thus making the president of the Louisiana Senate, Alvin O. King, the acting lieutenant governor and the successor to Long when he finally did take his oath as senator from Louisiana. Cyr died in August 1946.

Benjamin "Benny" Blakeman, nephew of Ada Leboeuf and son of the Morgan City chief of police, was later elected clerk of court for St. Mary Parish, serving in that position from 1952 to 1984. He died in Morgan City in May 1997.

James Monroe Beadle was released from the Louisiana State Penitentiary at Angola in April 1939. His wife had died and what remained of his family was scattered and destitute. He died a few years after his release.

Index